OPTIMIZING THE ORGANIZATION

OPTIMIZING THE ORGANIZATION
How to Link People and Technology

EMILY E. SCHULTHEISS

BALLINGER PUBLISHING COMPANY
Cambridge, Massachusetts
A Subsidiary of Harper & Row, Publishers, Inc.

International Standard Book Number: 0-88730-305-6

Library of Congress Catalog Card Number: 88-24249

Printed in the United States of America

Library of Congress Cataloging-in-Publication Data

Schultheiss, Emily E., 1949–
  Optimizing the organization.

  Bibliography: p.
  Includes index.
  1. Organizational effectiveness.   2. Organizational charge.   I. Title.
  HD58.9.S38   1989   658.4'063   88-24249
  ISBN 0-88730-305-6

To Arthur,
who has always believed in me

CONTENTS

LIST OF FIGURES

PREFACE

The world is changing. Our competitors are no longer down the road or across the street; they are scattered across the globe, flooding our markets with products undreamed-of several decades ago. Our customers are demanding higher quality, better service, and lower prices. Our employees want meaningful work and a chance to control their destinies, as well as the tasks they perform. Shareholders want higher returns, which means lower costs.

Early in the decade, we began trying to meet the new challenges with plans for unmanned factories and flexible machining centers. But, as technology and customer demands began changing more quickly than ever before, we soon discovered that we needed more flexibility than could be supplied by expensive hardware. We have installed advanced manufacturing systems that link our engineering to our manufacturing, only to confront in many cases turf battles within the organization that diminish the effectiveness of the new technology. In some organizations, robots have enhanced productivity and reduced costs; in others, they sit idle, tributes to our initial enthusiasm for popular automation, now contributing only to our base of invested capital.

As managers and entrepreneurs, we have recognized that our past answers are no longer as effective today, but so far we have been short on new solutions. *Optimizing the Organization* is written for managers and business owners who understand the need for a different approach to making their organizations competitive in today's turbulent environment.

Using a sociotechnical systems approach to restructuring organizations for increased flexibility, quicker response time, and more effective use of both people and technology, *Optimizing the Organization* provides a practical guide for managers or entrepreneurs acting as change agents in their own organizations. Whether in a small, family-owned enterprise or a larger, more complex publicly held entity, managers at all levels will benefit from the straightforward approaches to analyzing the workings of their organizations and restructuring them to fit the overall purpose or mission.

In the past, the body of literature regarding sociotechnical systems was confined to academic treatises that gave the practicing manager or business owner little guidance on the actual application of these approaches. Time and again, I have heard managers lament that they needed a "cookbook" approach to sociotechnical systems.

Yet a "cookbook" could not possibly respond to the wide variety of organizations and situations that exist. Instead, *Optimizing the Organization* offers a practical approach that provides managers with enough information and understanding and sufficient latitude to apply the concepts effectively to their particular situations. Practical worksheets and checklists allow managers to structure their attempts to optimize their organizations.

There are good reasons why a guide such as this has been so long in coming. Managers and consultants who have forged their way through the difficult literature to emerge with a workable approach have preferred to share only the results of their efforts. The process itself has often been considered a competitive edge: If too many consultants share their tricks, their businesses may suffer; and, if managers share their experience, their competitors may catch up.

I have written this book in defense of sociotechnical systems to show that they provide a practical, workable approach to structuring an entire organization to be competitive in tumultuous circumstances. But I have also been driven by a conviction that, as we add increasingly more complex technologies to our already complex organizations, we need to simplify our structures in order to gain the most from both our new technology and our human resources.

The ability to design organization structures that optimize both the contributions of our human resources and the capabilities of our technology will be the key to success as our business environment becomes more turbulent, our customers more demanding, our competitors more numerous, and our resources scarcer.

ACKNOWLEDGMENTS

Writing a book is a very solitary endeavor, and I often felt cut off from the life that continued on around me. However, behind the scenes were scores of supporters who listened to my musings, related stories about their experiences in organizations, made suggestions, offered encouragement, and generally accepted patiently my preoccupation. While it is impossible to thank all those who played a role in bringing me to this point, I owe special thanks to the following: Marjorie Richman of Ballinger, who relentlessly pursued quality and forced me to do the same; Charles Geaney of University College, Dublin, who introduced me to sociotechnical systems and suggested the need for a practical application guide on the subject; Nell Hartley of Robert Morris College, who read the first draft of two chapters and encouraged me to continue; Larry Michaelsen of the University of Oklahoma, whose conversations with me over several months focused my thinking on sociotechnical systems and their role in organizational change efforts; all my colleagues at work—especially to Bob Nelson, whose experience has been considerable—who continually encouraged me to pursue the subject and related numerous examples and stories about their own organizational change experiences; Jennifer Ference, who helped me unlock the secrets of my wordprocessing software, and Chuck Fritz and Dick Trainor, who provided similar assistance with the hardware; my action-planning team at the Center for Creative Leadership's Leadership Development Program, who helped me set the goal for beginning this book; and, finally, Art and Joy, who kept things going and uncomplainingly demanded less of me while I was writing, which is no small contribution.

OPTIMIZING THE ORGANIZATION

1 UNDERSTANDING SOCIOTECHNICAL SYSTEMS AND ORGANIZATIONAL DESIGN

> For want of a nail, a horse was lost;
> For want of the horse, a rider was lost;
> For want of the rider, a battle was lost;
> For want of the battle, a war was lost;
> For want of the war, a kingdom was lost—
> And all for the want of a horseshoe nail.
> —Children's Nursery Rhyme

Several years ago, a colleague breezed into my office and dropped on my desk a page torn from a magazine. The full-page color photo showed a human hand grasping the pincers of a robotic arm.

"What's this?" I asked, puzzled.

"That," he answered with a twinkle in his eye, "is a sociotechnical system! Isn't that what you're interested in?"

Indeed, optimizing the relationship between people and technology had occupied my interest and my time for several years. The artist's handiwork in front of me spoke eloquently of that relationship. The two hands—one human, one mechanical—could have been clasped in a handshake of friendship or clenched in the preliminary grip of an arm-wrestling match. That simple, ambiguous pose depicted the uneasy connection between humans and technology, especially as they exist in organizations—at times, positive and synergistic; at other times, negative and diminishing the overall results of the organization.

The limitations of the magazine photo as a depiction of sociotechnical systems lay in its very simplicity. First of all, technology normally extends beyond robotics or even hardware to encompass work, work methods, and procedures in general. The very nature of organizations

1

is to get results through people using tools, processes, or technology. Second, the relationship between people and technology in organizations is not always clearly defined. In fact, the people-work relationship and the difficulty of calibrating it are often a manager's greatest challenge. As technology changes, this people-work relationship becomes more important, not less. According to a *Business Week* study, the more advanced the technology, the more attention must be paid to an organization's people (Hoerr 1986). Some managers now speak of the high-tech/high-touch connection in organizations with advanced technologies. Unfortunately, that connection is neither as clear as the magazine illustration of the two hands, nor the old nursery rhyme that traces the loss of a kingdom back to the loss of a horseshoe nail.

SOCIOTECHNICAL SYSTEMS: INTEGRATING PEOPLE AND TECHNOLOGY

As managers, when we need improvement, we tend to focus on one thing at a time. We fix a technical problem. Then we fix a people problem. Then we adjust another technical problem. At the end of a day at work, we feel like jugglers. In many ways, we are just that.

The old television variety shows presented ample opportunities for us to watch juggling acts. These acts fell into two broad categories: plates on poles or objects in the air. The plates-on-poles jugglers set up a series of poles, each with a spinning plate. They started one plate and pole at a time, moving back and forth along the row, attending to each pole only when its plate began to slow down and it was in danger of falling. The objects-in-the-air jugglers worked with all the objects at once, continually rotating them in a coherent pattern that gave equal attention to each.

As managers, we often operate more like plate-on-a-pole jugglers, attending to each aspect of our organizations only when a need arises. Because some of the "plates" require more attention than others, we cannot see the connections between events and pieces in our organizations.

In many U.S. firms these days, you can almost hear the crash of plates dropping to the ground as managers run frantically from pole to pole, trying to keep more plates spinning than their counterparts in their competitors' organizations. We make improvements in one area, hoping to optimize our organizations, often to discover that we have created an imbalance and our situation is no better—and some-times even worse—than it was before we began.

Increasingly, we need to be able to provide the quick responses necessary to remain competitive in a changing environment with continually advancing technology. For that reason, the organization must be structured so that people and technology can both be optimized and, in turn, respond quickly to feedback from the environment and from their own activities.

The Origins of Sociotechnical Systems

The sociotechnical systems approach that integrates people and work to optimize overall results was born of a similar need to find the right balance. In post–world War II England, automation and new work methods were introduced into the coal mines to improve productivity. The result of this technological "improvement" was an alarming drop in productivity. Management enlisted the help of two consultants, Eric Trist and Kevin Bamforth, to tell them why. The key lay in the connection between the people in the organization and the work they performed (Trist and Bamforth 1951).

Under the old mining method, a small three- to four-man crew would spend an entire shift performing all the tasks necessary to tunnel, blast, shore up, and retrieve coal from a short section of a mine wall. They could adjust their activities to conditions at any given point in the mine at any given point in time. They could pass information on to the next crew, who could then take up where they left off. This method, however, did not allow optimal usage of the long, narrow coal deposits that were typical of British mines. As a result, new technology was developed that would allow maximum extraction.

New Work Methods. With the technology, came new work methods. Larger crews performed specialized functions, such as tunneling, building track, blasting, or retrieving coal. Each crew performed its specialty for an entire shift along the length of a mine wall. In every twenty-four-hour period, crews on two shifts spent their time preparing the coal for retrieval and shoring up the walls and roof to prevent collapses. A third shift did nothing but retrieve coal. If the area had not been properly prepared by the first two shifts, the retrieval efforts suffered; sometimes, the extraction shift could not work at all.

New Reward Systems. To further complicate matters, the preparation teams were paid at various rates according to the tasks performed. The people who drilled holes for the blasting were paid by the numbers of holes dug. The people who undercut and cleaned out beneath the blasting area so that the coal would have some place to fall were paid by the yard. Those who tore out the tunnels and shored them up were paid by the cubic measure of area prepared. Several specialties were paid straight wages based strictly on the hours worked. Finally, those who retrieved the coal were paid by the tonnage.

If the holes were not drilled properly for blasting, the coal was not loosened adequately, which hampered the workers who retrieved it. If the undercut was not made and cleaned out properly, the coal had nowhere to fall, and, again, those who retrieved coal found their efforts frustrated. Feedback to those who drilled holes or did the undercutting or tunneling came only after the retrieval shift discovered problems stemming from poor preparation.

New Structure. The new method changed more than the design of the work; it also changed the structure of the organization from small goal-oriented groups to larger task-conscious groups. Under the new system, if the task could not be performed under existing conditions in the mine, workers simply could not function, and received no pay, most likely, until the next shift. Instead of rewarding everyone based on the amount of coal retrieved from the mine, which would have been congruent with the mine operators' goals, only one group was rewarded on that basis. The others were rewarded for performing their specific tasks, even if the manner in which they did so contributed nothing to the overall objective of extracting coal from the mine.

The connections between the people in the organization and the technology or work method used had broken down—not so much because of the new technology, but because the new structure and reward system had been designed with *only* the technology in mind.

Linking People and Technology. After the problems in the coal mines were discovered, experts began to think more about how to link an organization's people with its technology or work methods so that they could optimize the organization's ability to achieve its goals or mission. The term "sociotechnical systems" was coined to describe this approach: "Socio" referring to the human aspects of the organization; "technical" referring to the mechanical or work aspects of the organization; and "systems" because of the interaction between people and work and the concept's dependence on the notion of an organization as a system, particularly an open system.

THE ORGANIZATION AS AN OPEN SYSTEM

Many metaphors have been used to describe organizations (Morgan 1980, 1986). At its simplest, the open systems metaphor compares an organization to a living organism. It assumes that the organization is able to interact with and adapt to its environment and maintain a healthy internal balance. Entities and situations outside the organization can affect what happens within it, and the organization, in turn, can influence what happens in and around it.

In today's turbulent business environment, only organizations that adapt can survive. Older metaphors described organizations as efficient machines, an analogy that worked fairly well in more stable business environments. Each part of the organization served a single specific purpose. Managing a mechanical organization involved keeping it well oiled and ensuring that all parts functioned properly. If today's managers continue to think of their organizations as machines, they will find themselves spending so much time redesigning the machines to do things that they were not originally intended to do and replacing parts that may not be interchangeable that the machine may not run often enough to produce any output. Today's environment demands a more organic, flexible model. The sociotechnical systems approach provides that flexibility.

The Open Systems Model

In an open systems model, the organization takes in information from its environment and adjusts its activities to meet the challenges of the market or continually changing business conditions. Meanwhile, internally, the people aspects and the mechanical or technical aspects of the work are balanced to provide optimum results.

Under the open systems model, organizations are seen as taking inputs from the environment, using some process to transform them into outputs, and returning those outputs to the environment. Along the way, feedback results from by-products of the transformation process and the outputs. The system is considered to be open because the model recognizes that the environment can influence the organization, either through the inputs that enter the transformation process, or through the transformation process itself, often by placing constraints on the elements of production or by imposing rules on the use of labor or outlawing certain chemicals or processes, for instance. Figure 1–1 is a graphic representation of the open systems model.

Transformation Process.   An open systems model tends to focus on the transformation process within the organization. This process includes the activities that the organization performs to earn its profits; it reflects how the organization goes about transforming raw materials and information into goods and services. It is here that the technology of the organization must come together with the people of the organization to get work done. Most managers and entrepreneurs find this focus on action to be appealing.

Inputs and Outputs.   Despite the tendency to concentrate on the transformation process, it is only one element of the open systems model of organizations. The model begins with inputs to the organ-

Figure 1–1.   Open Systems Model.

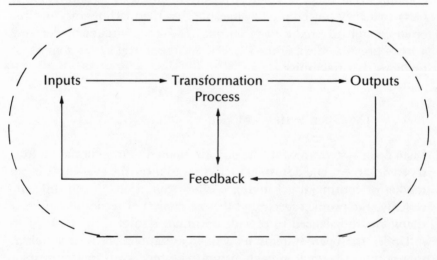

Inputs   ⟶   Transformation   ⟶   Outputs
Process

Feedback

Environment

ization: labor, raw materials, information, capital, and so forth that come into the organization from its environment. These inputs are combined in the transformation process to create the organization's outputs, the products of the organization, including any unwanted by-products that may result from the transformation process.

Often, outputs can indicate when an organization's people and work elements are out of balance. In the English coal mines, the fact that less coal came out of the mines after the technological improvements were made alerted management that something was wrong. In the United States in the last few years, declining output or stagnant productivity has raised the red flag for a number of organizations.

Until relatively recently, managers were not encouraged to spend much time or energy on the inputs or outputs of the organization; the focus was still on changing the transformation process. In the last few years, however, as customers have demanded higher quality, both inputs and outputs have taken on new importance. More emphasis is placed on relationships with both vendors (the suppliers of many inputs) and customers (the receivers of outputs, the suppliers of inputs in the form of orders, and the suppliers of feedback).

Feedback.   Feedback is information that is used to keep the organization balanced and functioning well within its environment. Feedback often results from the output and goes back into the transformation process to provide information about the way the organization works. Feedback about the organization's inputs can also result from the transformation process. Sometimes the transformation process itself can be designed to provide feedback to keep its own workings in balance.

Organizations as Multiple Open Systems

An organization may be viewed as a single open system, in which inputs are transformed into outputs, receiving feedback along the way. Most organizations, however, are described more accurately as containing multiple transformations, sometimes connected to each other by inputs, outputs, and feedback, as in Figure 1–2, and sometimes disconnected, operating with only random dependence on each other, as in Figure 1–3.

In the first instance, the output from one transformation process

Figure 1–2. Open Systems Model with Sequential Transformation Processes.

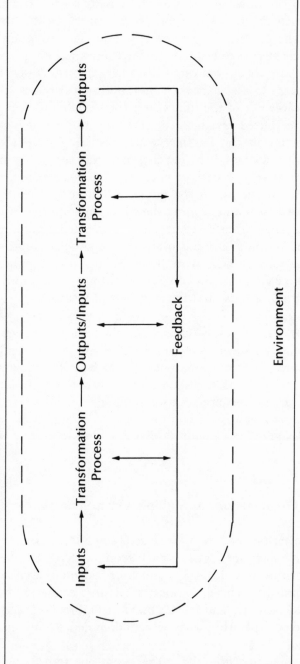

Figure 1–3. Open Systems Model with Multiple Transformation Processes.

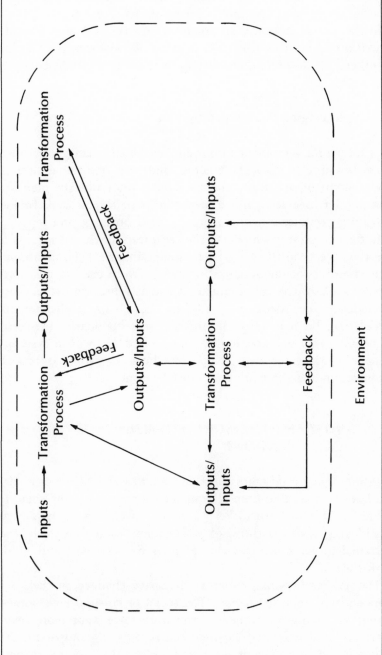

9

becomes the input for another. For a manager of a single transformation process, the larger organization itself becomes part of the environment—often the most important environment.

In the second instance, an organization may deal with several unrelated products or services. The outputs of some may provide inputs for others, while some units may operate relatively independently.

Managing in an Open System

Let's return for a moment to our analogy of the manager or business owner as a juggler. As we have noted, under the traditional mechanical model of the organization, the manager is more like the plates-on-a-pole juggler, operating like a mechanic, repairing what is broken or providing preventive maintenance to avoid breakage and repairs.

In the open systems model of the organization, the manager is more like the objects-in-the-air juggler, maintaining a balance among the various aspects of the organization and between the organization and the demands of the environment, constantly listening to and acting on feedback. The manager's job focuses less on single elements in the model than on managing the interfaces or boundaries between the elements. In an organization being operated as an open system, the manager works continually to optimize both the people aspects of the organization and the work that must be done.

WHY AN INTEREST IN OPTIMIZING THE ORGANIZATION?

Juggling of any kind takes effort. If, as a business owner or manager, you have been able to keep all your plates spinning, why should you suddenly want to learn to keep a variety of objects in the air? Why should you begin to think of your organization differently and to rearrange its structure to create a closer fit between people and the work they do?

The answer lies in three areas that have changed in the last few years and continue to change. The social or cultural environment is changing. Younger members of the work force want more than the treatment or benefits that satisfied their parents or grandparents. Technology is evolving. The products and services that we provide and the ways in which we generate them are changing more rapidly all the time. The business environment has become more competitive. The economic world has shrunk, and our competitors are often on the other side of the world in places that we never even thought about ten years ago.

Social or Cultural Imperatives

In terms of social or cultural trends, suffering is "out." It may never have been "in," but, until the last generation or so, a lot of people took it more or less for granted—it was an accepted part of living. While many people still suffer, those in the work force generally have less tolerance for uncomfortable, unrewarding work than their parents or grandparents did.

Breaking Down Work Led to Work Breakdowns. Early in the twentieth century, thanks in large part to the work of Frederick Taylor, skilled work that may have been rewarding in itself began to be broken down into discrete, loosely connected tasks or functions. Individuals became little more than replaceable parts in the great machinery of the organization. Ultimately, this division of labor began to cause stagnation: An individual tightening bolts on a factory floor or processing paper in an office often has so little connection to the organization's overall goal or mission that there is small incentive to improve performance. If you do not know what the goal is, it is difficult to set out to reach it more quickly.

In the early 1980s I encountered an example of this disconnection from the organization's overall goal. I was working with a group of secretaries to middle managers in an organization that provided support and consulting services, primarily to manufacturing groups. The secretaries were trying to improve their performance, which would, in turn, improve the overall organization. The organization was small enough that any of them might have been expected to know exactly what was happening in any part of the organization and to see how their collective and individual improvements would benefit the larger organization. However, after a while, their comments made me suspect that they had little idea why they were in business. Finally, I asked them what their organization did. There was a moment of silence, and then one young woman answered that they painted things. The others looked at her incredulously. "Well, we must paint things," she concluded, "because all I've done since I've been here is type up paint specifications and order paints. Why else would we be ordering all that paint?"

From the turn of the century until the last decade or so, millions of employees have been content to work at jobs that might have led them to believe that their organizations was in the business of making subassemblies or shuffling paperwork. Like the blind men describing the elephant, they were blocked from understanding the organization's purpose by their narrow focus on only their part of it.

Changing Labor Conditions. Today's employees are not so docile. They want to know why they are working, and they want to have a part in the overall process. They want to know that what they are doing is worthwhile, and they want jobs that make sense. Above all, they want some control over their destinies.

So far, organizations have been able to ignore these demands from their employees. High unemployment rates have limited individuals' power to make their demands heard and heeded by making it easy to replace workers who complain too loudly. However, the labor supply will not be so abundant in the future; indeed, there will likely be shortages as a result of the "baby dearth" of the sixties and seventies.

Scarcity may also be expected to drive the cost of labor higher. The wage concessions of the eighties may dissolve in the face of labor shortages. Accomplishing the same work with fewer people may become an imperative rather than an attractive goal.

Already, the need to reduce employee costs has motivated some industries to pay more attention to the people, or social, aspects of their organizations in attempts to use more fully the human resources they have available or, in some cases, a smaller number of people than in the past. Some have discovered that listening to complaints and giving people more control over their work has resulted in better quality and productivity.

Technological Imperatives

When technology was applied to the discrete tasks that individuals performed, new methods often did not disturb the internal balance of the organization. For example, substituting a power drill for a hand drill allowed the operator to work faster, without changing that person's relationships with others in the organization.

New technologies, however, are increasingly more complicated and less discrete than their predecessors. Consider, for example, the introduction of a robot into an organization. Often a robot performs a fairly simple task: moving parts or equipment from one place to another, welding or bolting parts together. Yet the installation of a robot generally involves some redesign of work flow. Layouts often must be rearranged. Sometimes, parts are redesigned to accommodate the relatively limited capability of a robot.

At this point, far more than the worker who was doing that job is being affected. Industrial or manufacturing engineers are involved in the new layout of the work area. Design engineers may become involved if parts must be redesigned to accommodate automatic handling. At some point, the maintenance department must become involved to learn how to repair the new equipment. In many cases, the maintenance department must accept a new priority for regular preventive maintenance, since the delicate hydraulics of many robots will not tolerate neglect.

Robots are only the beginning of the story. Advanced manufacturing systems that use computers to link the design function directly to the production function will eventually force organizations to reconsider the traditional separation of engineering and manufacturing into discrete departments. The more integrated our technology becomes, the more we must concern ourselves with internal balances and integration.

Leveraging Technology for Success.   As the various functions within an organization become linked by technology, the roles of the individuals performing those functions change. As a result, the structure of the organization must also change to maintain the internal balance. Success depends on a structure that allows advanced technologies to provide the maximum possible leverage and individuals to use the technologies to their full potential.

Business Imperatives

Today, the pressures of being first in the marketplace with new products already are forcing a reassessment of the way we have structured our organizations traditionally. When an automotive company had the luxury of taking up to five years to design a car and build the prototype, the marketing, engineering, and manufacturing functions could operate as separate departments. Now, to compete with the flexibility that foreign manufacturers have introduced into the marketplace, most automobile companies are discovering that they must reduce the time of that cycle. The engineering team can no longer toss their new design, like a grenade over the wall, to a waiting manufacturing group who only then can discover whether the product is produceable. Product teams that integrate the various functions involved in designing, marketing, and producing are becoming less and less just "a nice thing to do" and more and more the only way to survive.

Quicker Response Time.   The need to be first in the marketplace also reduces the time organizations have for making standard decisions. Organizations that have been heavy with layers of managers, each of whose approval was required for anything to get done, are falling behind in the race to be first. Top managers are finding that they can no longer afford the luxury of dictating the details of how work should be done. They have time only to scan the horizon for new opportunities and make their visions and intentions clear to those who are sailing the ship. The details of who stokes the boiler and who feeds what kind of food to the crew must be left to those lower in the organization.

Only an organization structured to optimize both people and technology can provide the quick responses required by today's challenging, ever-changing technological and competitive environment.

SOCIOTECHNICAL SYSTEMS AND ORGANIZATION STRUCTURE

In recent years, the application of sociotechnical systems approaches has often been limited to the design and redesign of work, rather than encompassing the structure of an organization as a whole. Volvo used a sociotechnical systems approach to redesign their work in Kalmar, Sweden, replacing routine, repetitive jobs on moving assembly lines with group assembly tasks in which a team of people was responsible for the manufacture of an entire automobile or subassembly. This application has had generally positive outcomes. Meaningful jobs were created. The work itself now provides feedback, so that complicated, costly control systems can be eliminated. Problems can be solved more quickly, because most of the people involved work together on a regular basis. The changes instituted at Kalmar resulted in a 25-percent reduction in production costs compared to such costs at Volvo's conventional plants (Hoerr 1986). U.S. auto makers that have moved to more flexible, participative structures have managed to maintain their output with about half as many people (Bernstein and Zellner 1987).

While this meshing of the individual with the task through work design and redesign is certainly an important aspect of a sociotechnical systems approach, these limited applications ignore the power of sociotechnical systems to integrate people and technology. New technologies and competitive pressures are now forcing managers to look beyond this narrow work design application to the structuring or restructuring of a total organization.

A Practical Approach

The remainder of this book will be devoted to applying a sociotechnical systems approach to an organization's structure. You may want to begin by doing the application activity in Figure 1–4, either alone or with your staff.

We will look at a sociotechnical systems approach in four broad phases. The first phase is *decisionmaking*, where we will examine the decisionmaking process that leads an organization to embark on a sociotechnical systems design project. The level of commitment required to redesign an organization successfully makes this definition of purpose a crucial first step.

The second phase of a sociotechnical systems approach is *analysis*. This will enable you to analyze your own organization to decide the best way to proceed or even to decide whether a redesign is necessary. Many organizations press on with implementation without making a conscious decision to do so. In some cases, discretion would have been the better part of valor.

The third broad phase in a sociotechnical systems redesign is *implementation*. No matter how much is written—or read—about implementation, the initial plunge will always feel somewhat like that first high dive. But there are some pointers that can make the going easier and more deliberate than just jumping off the board and hoping for the best.

Figure 1–4. Application Activity.

In considering whether a sociotechnical systems approach would be appropriate for your business or organization, ask yourself the following questions. You may want to solicit the input from others within your organization.

Social or Cultural Issues
   Do people at all levels of my organization understand enough about the business as a whole to be able to contribute to a continuous improvement effort?
   Are conflicts for resources resolved at the level where they occur, or do they come further up the organization, perhaps all the way to me?
   What kind of labor turnover have we experienced in the last two years? Do we lose the people we want to lose, or do we lose key contributors?

Technological Issues
   What new technology have we installed in the last five years? Have the improvements lived up to our expectations? If not, why not?
   What new technologies have we avoided? Why?
   Do our latest technological improvements belong to the category of "discrete technology," like an automatic drill or electric typewriter, or would they be classified as "integrated," like a CAD/CAM system, robots, or an automated manufacturing system?

Business Issues
   How quickly can we respond to marketplace changes compared to our competitors? Compared to what our customers would like to see?

The last phase of a sociotechnical systems application is *follow-up*. Few managers will want to continue a design that is not working, so we will discuss measurement and monitoring. We will also explore other aspects of the organization's system that may need to change to make a redesign effort successful, such as reward systems, the roles of managers and nonmanagers, training, and skills necessary in the new structure.

While a broad application of sociotechnical systems requires greater commitment and support than the redesign of work alone, it can produce results that will help an organization move successfully into the future. When you integrate the human and technical aspects of your organization so that they are able to respond to changing customer demands, increased competition, and a turbulent environment in general, you can truly optimize your organization.

2 TAKING THE FIRST STEPS TOWARD SUCCESS

A journey of a thousand miles must begin with a single step.
—Chinese Proverb

The first step toward optimizing people and technology and the work they do together in your organization is to make a conscious decision to do so. Then, once you have chosen to tread the path of organizational restructuring, you must make some specific decisions about how to begin in your own organization—what steps you must take to increase your potential for success, whose help you should enlist along the way, and how you should go about gaining the necessary commitment at all levels of the organization.

TO CHANGE OR NOT TO CHANGE

Most managers can look back on their careers and point to a series of successes that have brought them to where they are today. Because you want the restructuring of your present organization to add to that list of successes, you will want to think through the design project before you begin, asking yourself a series of questions about the decision you are about to make. Among these questions are:

- What are your reasons for wanting to redesign your organization using a sociotechnical systems approach?
- What is your potential for success?

- How much commitment already exists for such a change?
- What is the outcome that you expect personally?

In this chapter, we will consider each of these general questions and their related issues. The accompanying figures provide guidelines for approaching the answers to these questions. Managers who answer these questions candidly will have a sounder basis for deciding whether to proceed with the restructuring of their organizations, as well as a clearer vision of where they are going and what the path ahead looks like.

Identifying Your Organization's Needs

Different organizations face different challenges, from both environment and their current internal structures. In Chapter 1, we discussed some of the general forces that may push organizations to apply a sociotechnical systems approach to restructuring:

- Social or cultural changes, such as those occasioned by the new generation of workers, apparently meaningless, disconnected tasks, and a declining labor supply.
- Technological changes, such as more complex technologies that require greater integration of an organization's previously separate functions.
- Business changes, such as increased competition, the need for constantly updated products, and increased customer demand for higher quality.

Although most organizations face similar broad challenges, many would define their needs differently. The individual needs you identify can give you some indication whether restructuring is a sound option. These organizational needs become the compelling reasons for undertaking a restructuring effort.

A Tale of Two Organizations.   The case of two organizations that were considering using a sociotechnical systems approach for very different reasons offers an illustration of how perceived needs can vary. The first organization produced material that was used in the construction of nuclear reactors. Looking ahead, they saw their near-monopoly being threatened by the entrance of two foreign competitors into the market—both at lower prices. They also saw that they could remain competitive only if they could become both more productive and more flexible to meet the demands of their customers. As a result, they determined to implement a sociotechnical systems approach.

The second organization made heavy equipment, with special emphasis on the electronic systems to control the equipment. They, too, were facing stiff competition, accompanied by declining business that had forced numerous layoffs over a several-year period. They identified a need for a less rigid employee-transfer procedure to handle these layoffs, so that they could lay off workers without worrying later about who moved to what job. They considered using a sociotechnical systems approach to create flexible work teams that could close the ranks and carry on as usual each time the workforce was cut. However, because they identified their needs so narrowly, they decided ultimately to write a new employee-transfer policy instead of restructuring the entire organization to accommodate a single symptom of increased competition.

There are two lessons to be learned from this tale of two organizations. The first is that your organization's needs must be identified as close to the root of the problem as possible. In the second organization, transferring people around after each layoff was a result of declining business in the face of stiffer competition. Yet they chose to label the symptom of frequent layoffs as their driving need. Treating the symptom led to a very different solution than if they had gone a step or two further and confronted the issue of declining business and increased competition.

The second lesson is that, if the organization's needs are not systemwide, a narrower, more limited solution may be in order. For example, in the second organization, when they identified their problem (rightly or wrongly) as being an inflexible employee-transfer policy, the simple way to solve that problem was to create a less rigid policy, which they did. Restructuring the entire organization merely to achieve that goal would have been like trying to cure a cold with a shot of penicillin. Not only would its effectiveness have been questionable, such a dramatic solution could have caused an unnecessary shock to the system.

Probing for Causes.   One helpful hint for getting to the real root of your organization's needs is to continue to ask "why" for every problem that is presented. In the second organization, for example, the probe may have gone something like this:

We need to restructure our organization.
Why?
We are spending too much time training people to do new jobs.
Why?
We are having too many layoffs.
Why?
Our business is declining.
Why?
Our competition is getting more of our business.
Why?
Their costs are lower and their quality is higher.
Why?
They make more effective use of their resources than we do.

At last, we come to a reason that would justify restructuring: making more effective use of human and technical resources; optimizing the integration of the two to make the organization more effective, more successful in achieving its mission. This is what a sociotechnical systems approach is all about.

Determining Your Potential for Success

There exist within many of us two competing impulses when we contemplate the possibility of change. The first arises when we look around us and see that many of our counterparts are taking innovative approaches to improve their organizations—the fear of being left behind can drive managers to adopt changes. The popular press is full of stories of organizations that are applying sociotechnical systems approaches to redesign the work that they do. Teams are springing up in places as unlikely as steel mills and automobile assembly plants. Successful managers do not want to find themselves still at the starting line when the dust clears.

Mitigating against the drive to grab some of the glory is an innate or learned aversion to risk. Change always involves some degree of risk. The key to managing risk is never to apply a more powerful solution than you need—put simply, never to risk more than you can gain—always to take positive action to minimize risk. Later in the chapter, we will talk about some specific positive approaches to minimizing risk, such as creating and communicating a clear vision, gaining commitment, and enlisting the help of others.

The Dangers of Change as a Last Resort.   Unfortunately, some managers take a more passive approach to minimizing the risk inherent in change by waiting until a situation is so dire that staying the same may involve a greater risk than making a change. While waiting until change is the last resort may make action appear less risky, the situation at that point is usually beyond control, and the opportunities for success are limited.

The greatest drawback to a last-resort approach to organizational change is that, by then, one of your most valuable resources will likely be in short supply. That resource is time. Rearranging boxes on a chart may be accomplished overnight; performing an adequate analysis to ensure that the new structure will be optimum for your business and your internal conditions takes more time. When the business itself is in serious trouble, time tends to be used to fight fires, rather than to perform careful analysis and planning for the future.

Maintaining Control over Time.   The time necessary for a successful restructuring effort will vary from organization to organization. Changes in smaller organizations generally take less time than changes in larger organizations, for a variety of reasons. First of all, there is less to change. Second, smaller organizations are usually less complex than larger organizations, so the analysis and planning can be done more quickly. Finally, there are fewer people whose commitment is required. Usually, the closer your organization is to the last-resort scenario, the less control you will have over the timetable. Even if you have plenty of time to perform the analysis and make the changes, your newly structured organization may not have time to prove itself. You may run out of time before you build the successful track record that your shareholders, your upper management, and your customers will want to experience as proof that your optimized organization is performing as they expect. For this reason, beginning the change effort as soon as you have articulated your organization's needs, before your situation becomes that of a last resort, is essential to a successful outcome.

In general, the more you can control the timetable without too many intervening influences, the easier your potential success will become. Involving more people to do the legwork required for analysis will cut down on the length of time spent but not necessarily on the total hours.

Level of Commitment

The third broad area you need to consider in deciding whether to pursue a sociotechnical systems approach to restructuring your organization is the expected level of commitment to undertaking such a change. In other words, how much do people at all levels *want* to see changes within the organization?

Later in the chapter, we will examine ways to gain commitment to the change. When making the initial go/no-go decision, however, you need to make a quick assessment of how much effort it will take to gain the commitment that you need and whether you can afford to expend that level of effort.

Commitment to Excellence.   Commitment from all levels and functions of the organization is critical to a restructuring effort. As you will see later, many areas will need to be involved to support the changes. New measuring systems may need to be developed, which will involve the financial organization. New compensation systems may need to be instituted, which will involve the human-resource experts. New relationships may be created between traditionally separate functions, such as marketing, manufacturing, and engineering. In many cases, managers will take on new roles as decisionmaking is forced lower and lower in the organization to gain flexibility and reduce response time.

Restructuring your organization using a sociotechnical systems approach ultimately may mean thinking about your mission and goals in new ways. It means optimizing every aspect of your organization so that you can excel in your mission. Excellence requires commitment. You and everyone in your organization must want to be the best that you can be.

Continuous Improvement as a Way of Life.   Your organization's history and culture will give you some clues about the existing desire for change. The best indication may be found in the general attitude toward improvement. In some organizations, continual improvement in all facets of their operations is a way of life. Everyone strives for improvement; innovation is encouraged. If your organization falls in this category, then restructuring to optimize the integration of people and technology will be, in many ways, business as usual. Living with change and continual improvements is what people expect.

Status Quo as a Goal.   In other organizations, more effort is spent in maintaining the status quo than in striving for improvement. Past changes and attempts at improvements have been poorly planned and introduced. Most of the changes that have been initiated have been allowed to fade away if they were not accepted immediately. This sort of history creates a "this-too-shall-pass" attitude among people at all levels in the organization. In these cases, attempts to optimize the organization will probably also result in business as usual, and changes will tend to be superficial and short-lived. Special attention must be paid to breaking out of past practices; sustaining the improvements and supporting the changes will take extra effort.

Expectations

People's expectations about the outcomes of restructuring may affect their commitment. Certainly, individuals who expect improvement in their own situations are likely to try harder to make the project a success. On the other hand, those who anticipate a lowering of status or a new unfamiliar role are likely to be less enthusiastic about the changes.

An exercise that you might want to do on your own is to make a list of all the results that you expect from restructuring your organization. Be as specific as possible.

_____

_____

_____

_____

As a point of departure for this exercise, you might want to study the items in Figure 2–1. These are some of the outcomes that have

Figure 2–1.   Possible Outcomes from a Sociotechnical Systems Approach to Organization Structure.

The process of "punching in and out" is eliminated at all levels, and individuals and groups become responsible for managing their own time to get the expected results.

Accounting information, such as monthly billings, expenses, and income before and after taxes, is shared with the entire work force.

A team of people from various levels and functions throughout the organization is given full authority to study the organization and recommend a new structure.

Final decision on the new structure is made jointly by you and a design team.

Supervisors function as facilitators rather than disciplinarians.

Problems are identified and solved by people at the point where they occur, rather than referred upward to you or your staff.

The total amount of money available for raises is allocated among teams and individuals based on performance and the judgment of team members.

Customers and clients meet directly with the people who are doing the work, rather than with customer-service specialists.

occurred in various organizations as a result of sociotechnical systems approaches. While none of these outcomes may result in your organization, you should decide before you begin whether you could live with results such as these.

You might also ask your key managers or staff members to list their expectations. Their lists may give you a clue as to the level of commitment or resistance you might experience later.

Greater Control with Less Supervision.   In one organization that had been operating for about four months under a new structure that involved semiautonomous work groups, one supervisor reported that, although it looked as though management had lost all control over the work, they had a better idea of where the product stood at any given point than they had ever had before. He was right. Prior to the change, production had shown variations of over 5,000 percent from one day to the next. Directing the tangled flow had been a nightmare for employees and managers alike. By the time the supervisor made this comment, the largest variation from the average daily production was closer to 40 percent, and even variations that large were becoming progressively rarer. At the same time, supervisors had ceased to be involved directly in overseeing the work, instead serving more as facilitators to help the teams get the work done.

Increased Productivity.   In the same organization, at about the same time, one team member was overheard to comment that it seemed as if no one was working nearly as hard as they used to and yet the product was flying out the door. He, too, was correct. Productivity over the period had improved 92 percent.

New Roles and Responsibilities.   The roles of nearly everyone in the organization had changed. Teams were controlling their own quality, tracking their own production, and meeting after work to identify and solve potential production problems. When material was late or defective, the purchasing department found itself answering directly to the group of people that needed it. The shipping department found that teams, interested in reducing shipping damages, wanted more control over how their products were packed. The controller found that he needed to generate numbers and measures that used not to be reported so that he could provide the teams with feedback on their performance.

One guaranteed result that you can expect is change. How much change depends on how far your organization was from an optimum condition. Not every organization that uses a sociotechnical systems approach winds up with teams or semiautonomous work groups; however, a lot of them do. We will explore some of the reasons when we talk about design in Chapter 4.

Identifying Your Biases.   If there are certain structures that you could not live with, you need to identify those configurations early and determine exactly why you would not want your organization to be structured in that way. If there are good business reasons for avoiding certain structures, a sociotechnical systems approach probably will not lead you to those structures. But if there are sound business reasons why one of those structures would be best for you, then you need to consider carefully your objections and biases in the matter.

A Few Sure Things.   Broadly, the certainties that you can expect are that you will experience change, that you will need to set aside sufficient time to complete an analysis before you determine what your new structure should look like, and that you will need the support of as many people as possible to make the restructure successful. Your own role is apt to change as you spend more time on strategic issues and less on day-to-day operations. The roles of many of your managers are likely to change as they become facilitators for accomplishing results, rather than overseers of operational details. The roles of non-managers will probably change, too, as they take on responsibilities for doing whatever it takes to achieve the organization's objectives.

Moving Ahead

Before you move ahead with a final decision, you may want to pause to be sure you have considered all the relevant issues.

Have you identified broadly the organizational needs that are driving you to make a change?

Have you weighed the overall potential for success based on your current circumstances and the amount of time you have to institute a change?

Have you assessed the current level of commitment to improvement?

Have you identified your own expectations for the new structure?

You may want to use the more detailed questions in Figure 2–2 to investigate these issues further.

The figure urges that you rethink your answers when they are not immediately positive rather than abandon the process. You will recall from the example of the two organizations earlier in the chapter that, if the second organization had considered their needs for change, they might have probed more deeply and decided to aim for an optimum

Figure 2–2.   Important Questions to Answer before Applying a Sociotechnical Systems Approach.

1. What are our reasons for wanting to use a sociotechnical systems approach to redesign our organization?
   A. Has the nature or composition of the work force changed? How?
   B. Has new technology been introduced? How is it working?
   C. Is new technology about to be introduced? What is it supposed to achieve?
   D. Has the marketplace changed for us? How?
   E. Is our competition more flexible than we are? Can they respond more quickly to their customers? Can we survive in our current mode?
2. What other organizations do we know of that have used a sociotechnical systems approach?
   A. How are they like us?
   B. How are they different from us?
   C. What can we learn from them?
3. How likely is our survival if we do not make any changes?
4. What kinds of resources can we commit to the change effort?
   A. Do we have enough time to make improvements or must we continue to put out fires?
   B. How much time are we willing to give ourselves to analyze what changes should be made?
   C. How much time are we willing to give ourselves to implement the appropriate changes?
   D. How much time will our customers or our shareholders give us to prove that we have improved our performance?
   E. What additional expertise will we need to complete the analysis? Are we willing to commit that expertise to the project?
5. How committed are we to the idea of organizational improvement?
   A. Can we make this task a priority for our people?
   B. How much authority are we willing to give to a design team in the early phases?
   C. How much commitment will we need from others in the organization? What is the best way to go about obtaining that commitment?

Figure 2–2.   cont.

6. What are our assumptions about why people work and what motivates people to do a good job?
  A. Do we believe that people will solve their own work-related problems if they are given the authority and the expertise to do so?
  B. What do we believe will happen in the short term if we design a more flexible organization? What do we believe the long-term effects will be?
  C. What are our worst fears about a new structure? Do our hopes outweigh our fears?

solution to their situation instead of a narrow approach to correct a symptom.

MOVING TOWARD A SUCCESSFUL APPLICATION

Once you have decided to apply sociotechnical systems to your organization, you must begin to think about how you are going to undertake this project. Getting off to a good start is critical to eventual success. To be sure you are heading in the right direction, you will first want to articulate a vision for your organization. Then, you must build commitment to your vision and to the change effort in general. Throughout these initial stages, you probably will not want to work alone; you will need to enlist the help of others.

Creating a Vision

One of the key elements in a flexible, optimized organization is that all members understand clearly the nature and purpose of the organization. This understanding is crucial because people will be using the organization's vision daily as a guideline as they make decisions about the best way to accomplish certain objectives. For example, if your vision involves becoming the low-cost producer in your field, people must know that, so that their decisions will be guided chiefly by the cost of various alternatives. If, on the other hand, your vision involves doing whatever it takes to provide the most outstanding customer service, operational decisions must be based on their predicted outcome for the customer.

Open Systems Planning.   One of the most effective ways to formulate a vision is to use a technique called "open systems planning" (Jayaram 1976). The exercise will provide you with a statement of your organization's overall mission, a vision of where the organization should be at some point in the future, and a broad idea of what kinds of actions you must take to reach that future.

Designed to be a group activity, this approach could be used well by you and your staff or key members of your management. The open systems planning approach can be especially useful for young businesses or for those who are just embarking on a new business venture. You will need to involve people who understand the nature of your business, your customers, and your environment.

Identifying Your Mission.   The first step in open systems planning is to identify your organization's mission. Some groups find this task very easy, because they have done it before and so are conscious of their mission and overall purpose. Other groups that have had little experience in this area may find that it takes a bit longer.

You may find this a worthwhile exercise, if only to discover that different people in the organization have different ideas about what the organization's purpose is. This task serves as an opportunity to begin framing the vision and making sure that the members of your staff, at least, are all heading in the same direction. You may use the box in Figure 2–3 to record your organization's mission.

Identifying Your Constituents.   Generate a list of all those individuals and groups that make demands on your organization, either internally or in the environment. You may find shareholders, employees, labor unions, government agencies, customers, the community, and so forth among those constituents. Identify what each group demands from your organization and be specific and accurate in generating this list. Figure 2–4 provides a convenient model for listing those constituents and their expectations or demands.

Accuracy in identifying the demands or expectations is particularly important. Often we discover that we have been operating under certain assumed constraints that may not exist at all. Many organi-

Figure 2–3. Organization Mission.

_____

```
┌─────────────────────────────────────────────────┐
│                                                   │
│   _____    │
│                                                   │
│   _____    │
│                                                   │
│   _____    │
│                                                   │
│   _____    │
│                                                   │
│   _____    │
│                                                   │
│   _____    │
│                                                   │
│   _____    │
│                                                   │
└─────────────────────────────────────────────────┘
```

_____

zations, for example, assume that the the government places certain constraints on them that often are not there. Organizations often assume that they are constrained from hiring qualified individuals because they must reach certain goals regarding female and minority placement. Such was never the intention of the equal employment opportunity law. Other organizations have avoided taking certain actions because they have assumed that labor unions would oppose them. Often these constraints are more imagined than real.

Generating this list may require some research in order to separate real from assumed demands. The entire process need not take place in a single meeting, so you can give people time to check out their assumptions between sessions.

Although this list will be set aside once it is generated, it will become valuable later when you begin considering actions to optimize your situation.

Looking toward the Future.   This step has several variations. You may find that one appeals to you more than another. Basically, you need to look at where you want to be at some point in the future, usually five years hence. Ultimately, the result of this step may be used as your vision.

Figure 2–4. Identifying Your Organization's Constituents and Their Expectations.

Internal Constituents		External Constituents	
Constituents	Demands	Constituents	Demands

The ideal future. Your look to the future should include a statement describing your organization's ideal future, covering the organization as a whole. You may also want to flesh out that statement with greater details about the workings of the organization. However, this statement will become your guiding vision—be careful about getting so specific at this point that your final version becomes a prescription instead.

This narrowing of the ideal future can occur in several ways. Say, for example, that you have decided that, in the ideal future, your organization will create additional value for your product by increasing quality and customer service. Many people could identify with this vision, and it could become a driving force for continuous improvement within the organization. One way for your future to telescope would be to envision a process rather than a position. Suppose that you flesh out this vision to the point of identifying exactly *how* you would improve quality. You articulate your vision as installing statistical process control in all departments and you state that quality will be improved by a specific percentage. This limits the amount of improvement you might get and the number of ways people might go about achieving it: No one need look further than your vision. By definition, you will reach your ideal future when you install statistical process control and achieve your designated percentage improvement. Additional value or customer service may or may not result.

A second way you can narrow the scope of your vision is to define a specific end product. For example, you may have your own ideas about what is causing your quality problems and you may even have developed a potential solution. If you articulate that specific solution, rather than the clear vision of creating value through increased quality, you will again limit the improvement you can get.

Likewise, if you are striving to improve response time and increase flexibility, you can limit your options too early by articulating a vision of semiautonomous work groups. Once you have your semiautonomous work groups, there is no more future to your vision.

Figure 2–5 provides space for you to record your ideal future or vision.

Figure 2–5.   Ideal Future.

If I look five years into the future, ideally, my organization should be

_____

_____

_____

_____

_____

_____

_____

Figure 2–6. Actual or Status-Quo Future.

If nothing changes within our organization, five years from now, we can expect to be _____

_____

_____

_____

_____

_____

_____

Examining the status-quo future.   After identifying their ideal future position, some groups choose immediately to see how they can get there. An interim step, however, may be useful. That step is to identify where you will be at the same point in the future if you change nothing, continuing to operate as you have operated and are operating now. This is sometimes referred to as the actual future. The benefit of this step is that it reveals clearly whether your current mode of operation is inadequate to move you into the future. When the gap between where you want to be and where you are likely to be is visible to the planning group, their concern about the future and their commitment to improvement generally rise a notch.

You can record your organization's actual or status-quo future in Figure 2–6.

Identifying this gap is well worth the time and effort that go into the exercise. Articulating where the organization is likely to be if you change nothing sometimes can supply the catalyst for taking action. On the other hand, if you discover that the future is bright and viable even if you make no changes, you may decide to leave things as they are.

Action Planning.   When you are using this technique to begin a sociotechnical systems approach to restructuring, you do not need detailed action plans—instead, you need an indication of the direction in which the organization must move in order to reach the ideal future. Some of the topics you address here may cause you to question further the need for restructuring. In most cases, however, the actions that you identify as necessary will probably confirm your need for a more effective structure. Either way, the exercise will be worthwhile.

Communicating Your Vision.   The results from the open systems planning activity are the basis of the vision that you must communicate to your entire organization. Without exception, everyone in the organization must understand this vision. (Ultimately, they must also believe in the vision and become committed to it, but this cannot happen without the initial understanding.) Clear and frequent communication is the key here.

Face-to-Face Communication.   The most effective communication is face to face. For this reason, you must be certain that every member of your management team can articulate the vision and does so frequently. Eventually, as others become involved in the change project, they, too, must become spokespersons for the vision. Your own conversations with others in the organization must reflect your commitment. They must know that the vision is more than fancy words that you included in some speech or letter or article in the house organ.

Actions Speak Louder than Words.   While the changes that you plan will not happen overnight, it is important that your actions begin to reflect your commitment to your vision. For example, if your stated aim is to become a low-cost producer, you should not follow that declaration with remodeling projects that turn the physical surroundings into a luxury resort. If your goal is greater flexibility to meet customers' needs more quickly, you should not follow the announcement of your vision with the introduction of new, rigid policies.

People will be watching your actions, and the actions of management in general, to see whether you are serious about introducing change. They will be unwilling to commit themselves to your vision if you do not demonstrate that you yourself are committed to its achievement.

Gaining Commitment

Making changes in a complex organization is not something that you can do alone. Nor can you monitor personally each person's actions to be sure that no one takes a false step. For that reason, you must have commitment from the members at all levels of your organization. Answering the questions in Figure 2–7 will clarify some of the issues you must address in order to gain commitment.

Figure 2–7.   Gaining Commitment.

- To whom must I justify any changes that are made?
- What sort of data or reassurances will sell them on the idea?

- What must be done to ensure that those directly involved can remain with the project throughout restructuring without missing valuable career opportunities?

- How do I demonstrate my own commitment?
- Are my actions consistent with my vision?
- Does my vision address the concerns of others in the organization?

Commitment from Above.   How much commitment you need from your boss and from upper management in general will depend on the degree of autonomy with which you operate and, possibly, your distance from the hierarchy above you. Certainly, your vision of your organization must be congruent with that of your boss or the shareholders. One way to ascertain this is to include these groups in your communications effort.

If you have a fair amount of autonomy and are located far from your boss, you may need little or no commitment from above. (Obviously, if you are the owner-manager of the organization, this question does not arise at all.) If you do need commitment from above, you must use whatever selling techniques that will help you gain that commitment.

If you belong to an organization where frequent transfers of managers are the norm, you may need a commitment from the overall organization that you and your key managers can remain in place during the analysis, implementation, and early operation of the new structure. This commitment should also include the promise that such immobility will not harm the careers of those involved.

Those above you in the organization may need some assurances that you know what you are doing, that such applications have worked before in similar organizations, and that you can indeed effect improvements through the action you are about to take. The results of your open systems planning may prove useful here.

Commitment from Below.   The first step in gaining the commitment you need from everyone involved in your own organization, both managers and nonmanagers, is to demonstrate that you yourself are committed. As we discussed earlier, this is done by communicating your vision and by beginning to live the vision. As the project gets under way and you begin to allocate resources to ensure its success, this demonstration of your own commitment will go far toward making believers of others in the organization.

One way to gain commitment from others in the organization is to make sure that they know that you understand their concerns about the current organization and the effect that any changes will have on them and their roles. This can be done when you communicate your vision. If your vision addresses some of their current and anticipated concerns, even in general terms, their level of comfort will increase.

If you are not sure of the particular concerns in the organization, listen to what people are talking about. This is an occasion when it pays not to have earned a reputation for shooting the messenger; if people expect you to react negatively to anything other than positive information, you may have difficulty discovering what their concerns are. Even then, however, others around you, either your peers or your immediate staff, may be more aware of the typical concerns of the organization's members.

ENLISTING HELP

Once people become committed to your vision, your next step is to put them to work. Very likely, you will have already included your staff or key managers in the open systems planning and mission statement activities. While it might be tempting to limit involvement to this group, which already has some experience in working together, normally they will not have enough detailed knowledge of the organization's operations or extra time to be able to carry the full load of the restructuring effort.

You must apply as much knowledge to the analysis and design as you can muster within your organization without jeopardizing your ongoing operations. For that reason, you will need to seek help from people at various levels and from various functions or areas of expertise within your organization.

You may also want to talk with managers of other organizations who have made similar changes or seek out consultants who have experience in the area of change, sociotechnical systems, or organization structures.

Forming a Steering Group

A steering group can be an invaluable resource in sociotechnical systems applications. Such a group comprises a number of knowledgeable people who understand both the way the current system actually works and the way it should or could work to achieve the organization's mission more successfully.

Role of the Steering Group.   The role of a steering group is literally to steer the restructuring project through the analysis and design phases and into implementation. In fact, the further you and your organization travel into uncharted waters, the more important your steering group will become. It can come up with fresh ideas and workable solutions to situations that you did not even anticipate when you began.

As the project progresses, you will need a reliable source of feedback on its status and effectiveness. If one of your goals is a more flexible organization, such feedback will continue to be important long after the initial changes have been made because constant adjustments may be necessary to respond to changing business needs or shifting market conditions.

Eventually, the steering group becomes a team of internal experts who come to know as much as, and perhaps more than, you do about how the organization operates, what the customers want, the nature of the organization's mission, the nature of sociotechnical systems, how people will react to the changes, how to increase further commitment at all levels of the organization, and how to monitor and maintain the new organization once it is in place.

Composition of the Steering Group.   The group should be large enough to be representative of the organization but small enough to be workable. Some organizations like to form their groups from a "diagonal slice" of the organization. If you drew a diagonal line through a traditional organization chart, you would intersect boxes representing various levels from various functional areas. A group formed of people from those positions would provide broad representation and perceptions from many points of view and experience from many different backgrounds.

Size. Six to twelve members is generally workable. If your organization is large, six may be too few, while more than twelve are difficult to manage. As your steering group gets under way with its analysis, members may want to recruit others to help with the legwork. Certainly, the more people become involved, the better information you will receive and the more commitment you will gain.

Membership Criteria. First of all, you should have a group with which you are comfortable. You have made an important decision in choosing to restructure your organization, and you must believe that the group you have working on analysis and implementation of that decision can fulfill such an assignment.

Second, you need a group that others will be comfortable having as their representatives. The rest of the organization needs to believe that their future is in capable hands. Having respected informal leaders in the group will become increasingly important as the project progresses. During the analysis phase, others in the organization must be able to trust those who are gathering data; otherwise, information will not be exchanged freely.

Finally, you need people in the steering group who will "tell it like it is" and not be timid about taking risks or assuming responsibility. You need group members who can work together on their own initiative, without your guidance on every step they take. You need people who will be candid and open and who will seek help when necessary.

Selection of Group Members. Several approaches may be used to select steering group members. The members can be handpicked, based on the criteria and parameters we have discussed or on others you consider to be important. The group may be staffed by volunteers who want to be part of the change process. Or you can use some combination of these two options. We will discuss further the advantages and disadvantages of each.

Calling for Volunteers. During my first experience with a sociotechnical systems application, the plant manager tossed aside the carefully prepared list of steering group candidates provided by the two consultants and said, much to our pleasure and surprise, that he would prefer to begin modeling participation in his organization simply by calling for volunteers to staff the group. His rationale was that he wanted only those people who really wanted to be involved. His vision of the new organization did not include continuing to order people to "volunteer." This rationale seemed so sound that we never stopped to critique its potential impact.

We discovered early that there were disadvantages to this free-for-all approach. For example, because we announced that the group was open to all volunteers, we had less control over size than we might have had. While this turned out not to be a problem in this case, we might have wound up with either too few or too many members.

A further drawback was that we had little control over the types of expertise and backgrounds represented by the volunteers. As a result, the group turned out to be somewhat deficient in terms of its business, technical, and human skills. A different organization might have turned up volunteers with a deeper level of skills and understanding; however, in many organizations, those whose plates are already full, so to speak, will not tend to seek more responsibility and involvement. You may get those who have little to do or those who normally are not chosen for task-force work or special projects because of lack of expertise.

Our greatest problem turned out to be the motivation of those who volunteered. Our assumption was that people would volunteer because they were interested in becoming involved in improving the organization. As it turned out, most of our volunteers were motivated more by a desire to control the situation and maintain the status quo than by a commitment to optimize the organization.

From the beginning, the list of volunteers surprised us. They tended to be individuals who had not taken an active part in the organization beyond performing their required tasks. They did not have records as outstanding contributors, and most were not even among the formal or informal leaders of the organization.

The result was that the project had to work around the steering group, rather than being guided by it. Separate groups were formed to analyze the data-collection results and propose new organization designs, as well as to create effective support systems for the new structure.

The ultimate lesson we learned was that there are distinct disadvantages to using unscreened volunteers when staffing a steering group but it is possible to adjust the situation to make the results livable.

Handpicking the Members. Handpicking the members of the steering group gives you greater control over the the group's final make-up. It allows you to control the size of the group, as well as the kinds and levels of expertise within the group. Alone or with the help of others within the organization, you can select a diagonal slice made up of representatives from various levels and functions.

The chief disadvantage to this approach is that you may end up with some unwilling or less-than-enthusiastic members. Not everyone will become equally committed equally as quickly to the idea of organization improvement. You may also overlook a few people who may be excited about your vision and really want to contribute to the change process.

The Best of Both Worlds. If neither approach seems quite right to you, you may want to devise a combination approach that will allow you to staff the group with the necessary expertise and at the same time include volunteers who might have a special desire to take part.

If you anticipate that a call for volunteers would draw so many people that the steering group would be unwieldy, you may want to call for volunteers first and then select members from that list using criteria appropriate for your situation.

On the other hand, if you believe that calling for volunteers would yield very few people, you might begin by handpicking some people for the group, based on appropriate criteria, and then fill the remaining slots with volunteers. You could even specify the departments, functions, or levels from which you want volunteers.

Another approach would be to work through your managers to staff the group, providing them with the criteria you want them to use in their selection. If a labor union is involved, you may want them to be involved in designing the selection procedure or criteria. At the least, you may want them to select some members from their own ranks.

Preparation of the Steering Group. Once you have selected your steering-group members, you must train them to work with a sociotechnical systems application. They will need to understand their charter, sociotechnical systems, and how this approach can be applied to the structure of an organization; they will need to learn to work together; and they may want to become familiar with other organizations that have made changes of similar nature or scope.

Understanding the Charter. The group must have a clear charter. For example, if you have already determined that a change is necessary, articulated your vision for the organization, and decided that a sociotechnical systems approach will work best, then the charter of the steering group is to carry out your decisions in the best way possible.

The steering group must understand your vision and your rationale for change better than anyone else in the organization, since they will be using your vision and rationale as the standard to evaluate all of their work. Everything they propose must be measured by how well it solves the problems that you have identified in a way that fits your vision of the organization.

They also need to understand your perception of their role in the change process. Will they only be overseeing the change process? Will they also be involved in data collection during the analysis phase? Will they be asked to propose new organization designs? These are questions that you may want to answer with the steering group, but the answers must be reached early in the process.

Several years ago, I ran into a situation that illustrates the importance of a clear charter for a steering group. This particular steering group was hampered at the outset by its size—thirty members strong. It had been meeting regularly for three months with no results to show for its efforts. The charter of this particular group had been to explore organizational change and sociotechnical systems applications, but, unfortunately, it had been given no clear vision of what top management had in mind when it was chartered.

As it turned out, management had not made a firm decision to make changes in the organization's structure. The group had been created simply to test the waters. Rather predictably, each side felt a lack of commitment on the part of the other. The steering group had no focus for any commitment it might generate. Top management had formed the group without being ready to commit to any particular change. Indeed, they never did commit to a sociotechnical systems approach, and, several years later, they began pursuing an alternate strategy. In the meantime, they rearranged the organization chart several times, much to the frustration of those in the boxes.

Understanding Sociotechnical Systems.   If you expect your steering group to follow a sociotechnical systems approach to analyzing and improving the organization, it follows that they must understand what this means. Reading, discussion, or talks by people who are knowledgeable in the area can be helpful here.

As group members begin to understand the process more fully, they will begin to teach each other. Allowing them to proceed in this manner not only will broaden their own knowledge, it will give them early experience in working with and supporting each other.

One way to help group members understand better how a sociotechnical systems approach might be applied to their own organization is to arrange for them to visit other organizations where similar changes have been implemented. Many firms are quite willing, even eager, to share their successes. Often, meeting with counterparts in another organization can be a powerful learning experience. These face-to-face visits also enable people to ask questions about their specific concerns, which may not be covered in magazine articles on the subject.

Enthusiasm is contagious, and steering groups often come away from these visits with more commitment and zeal than you could ever generate through discussions, lectures, or readings.

A well-staffed, well-prepared steering group can generate valuable commitment from others within the organization. Members also furnish the detailed knowledge of how the organization really works that is essential to a complete and accurate analysis, an effective design, and a successful implementation. Figure 2–8 provides a guide for you to use in setting up a steering group and preparing it to function.

Using a Consultant

Even the most confident managers sometimes seek outside help. The best time to bring in consultants is when you have little or no internal expertise in an area. In most organizations, this will probably be the case when they decide to apply a sociotechnical systems approach to restructuring.

If you decide to use a consultant, you should be sure that you stay in the area of using the consultant effectively, rather than relying so heavily on the consultant that you lose control of the project and fail to develop the level of understanding that a closer involvement would have brought. You, your managers, and the steering-group members need to stay involved in the project, retaining control of the activities in your own organization.

The Role of the Consultant. The first decision you must make is how you will use a consultant. Consultants can fill a variety of roles. Since you are the client, you should be able to choose the role and

Figure 2–8.   Steering-Group Checklist.

Formation of a Group

List the advantages you expect to gain by using a steering group.

List the activities you would expect a steering group to become involved in. (You may want to add to this list as you go.)

Composition

How large should your steering group be to represent your organization adequately?

If that size is too large, how else might you represent the various interests with fewer people?

What criteria are important for membership in your steering group?

Selection

If you called for volunteers, what would be the likely response, based on past experience?

If you handpicked the members, whom would you choose?

Whom would your staff recommend?

Preparation

In your opinion, what is the steering group chartered to do? (Be sure you include some information about your vision for the future in addition to the activities you expect the group to undertake.)

What must the group members understand about sociotechnical systems?

How will you see that they get this knowledge and understanding?

What other companies might you visit?

Who might come to talk about their own experiences to the group?

---

select a consultant based on his or her ability to fulfill it. If you go into the selection process with no particular role in mind, the chances are good that the consultant will make that decision for you. While this is not necessarily bad, most managers prefer more control.

Reference.   One possibility is to use the consultant as a living reference book, whose information will be transferred to you and the steering group during question-and-answer sessions and mini-lectures.

Catalyst.   A broader use of a consultant would for him or her to help you get started on the project "on the right foot," either in the decisionmaking phase or after you have made the decision. At this early stage in the project, the presence of a third party can provide some comfort, as well as guidance, both to you and to your steering group or staff members.

Challenger.   Another valuable use of a consultant is as an official questioner to challenge the assumptions on which you are operating, the decisions that you make regarding change, and the data that you collect—in short, to cause you to review all your past and current thinking about how things work both inside and outside the organization.

"Outside Eyes."   In general, if the role of a consultant could be summed up, it would probably be described as a pair of "outside eyes" that can look at the organization as no one inside it can. A consultant coming into an organization for the first time sees conditions with which those inside have grown so accustomed that they no longer notice them. This ability to bring a fresh outlook to your organization is one of the chief advantages of using a consultant.

Time Saver.   The consultant's previous experience with sociotechnical systems approaches may help you bring the new organization up to speed more quickly. An experienced observer can spot any potential pitfalls and steer you safely away from them before you are close enough to fall in.

Monitor.   A consultant also may serve to keep the change project or optimization effort on track. The application of a sociotechnical systems approach and the restructuring of the organization will become the consultant's chief interest in your organization. This means that he or she will continue to pull your attention back to the long-range design project when your operational crises threaten to distract you too much. When the alligators of day-to-day operations start nipping at your heels, the consultant will remind you that you need to be working on draining the swamp or those alligators will never go away. While consultants are sometimes criticized for their single-mindedness or narrow views, it is precisely this concentration that makes them valuable in keeping you on track.

Project Manager.   Sometimes, as in any project, it becomes tempting to use the consultant as a project manager. While the project ultimately may be very successful when handled this way, such arm's-length involvement on your part does not demonstrate commitment either to the process or to the final results.

Developing a Contract.   Contracts with consultants come in two forms: those that agree to methods and amount of payment and those that specify the consultant's role. The former tends to be more formal and written. The latter is usually less formal, often unwritten, and frequently overlooked. Whether or not your organization and the consultant require the formally executed document, you must be sure that you have clarified the consultant's role and what you expect in terms of consulting services.

Developing this role agreement, or contract of responsibilities, helps you retain control of the project and clearly defines the roles that both you and the consultant will play. Just as the steering group needs to understand its charter, so the consultant needs to understand your vision and expectations.

CONCLUSIONS

Making deliberate decisions early in the process helps you get the optimization project off to a good start. While the vision that you communicate will begin to steer the organization in the right direction, your actions will demonstrate your own commitment to the project more loudly than your words ever could.

Optimization is bound to bring change, and change, or talk of it, usually gets people's attention. From the moment change is contemplated, people will begin watching what you do, paying attention to how you go about planning the changes, and generally reading your actions to try to gauge whether you are truly committed to the vision you have created.

3 PERFORMING THE ANALYSIS

The best preparation for good work tomorrow is to do good work today.

—Elbert Hubbard, *The Note Book*, 1927

As managers, many of us have a penchant for action. As a result, one of the most tempting traps to fall into when redesigning our organizations is to skip analysis and jump right into design. After all, we are used to dealing with answers—they are our stock in trade. If you enjoy questioning, if you enjoy looking for information that you have never considered before, you will enjoy the analysis phase of organizational restructuring. If you prefer answers, you will be doubly glad that you have formed a steering group to follow the restructuring project because they can guide the analysis phase.

AN OVERVIEW OF ANALYSIS

Traditional sociotechnical systems methods use nine steps in the analysis process (Emery and Trist 1978).

1. Identifying the main characteristics of the production system and the environment, as well as the main problems so that the analysis can focus on these areas.
2. Outlining the main segments of the production operation.
3. Identifying "key process variances" and how they relate to each other.

49

4. Identifying and analyzing the social system of the current organization, including the structure of the current organization and the skills possessed by the workers.
5. Determining the extent to which people's current jobs fulfill their psychological needs.
6. Determining the nature of the maintenance operations and how they affect the production system.
7. Identifying the impact of suppliers and users on the production system and how these areas could be improved.
8. Identifying elements in the wider environment that affect the organization's ability to achieve its objectives or are likely to force changes in the objectives.
9. Developing proposals for change.

While these steps are fairly sound, they have received only the briefest description in existing literature. They are also geared primarily to a manufacturing operation and tend to focus more narrowly on the design of work, rather than the structure of the organization.

Here, we will look at seven steps, setting aside the proposals for change since we will cover those when we discuss the design phase, and modifying the others to encompass either production or service organizations. The steps are still based in large part on traditional literature and the work of Emery and Trist (1978) but also draw on practical experience and work done by others in the area of change and organization design (Tichy 1983; Walton and Susman 1987).

Broadly, we will cover these steps:

1. Preparing a broad statement of the current state of your organization. This statement should describe your current situation, your current economic conditions, and the concerns that are driving your desire to change.
2. Identifying the objectives of your organization, including the organization's outputs and major processes.
3. Identifying what normally goes wrong in the organization's processes. Included in this process is an explanation of exactly where these problems are found and how they are usually discovered.
4. Characterizing your organization's culture, including the beliefs and assumptions held by both management and employees as to how and why things work the way they do.

5. Identifying and outlining the formal and informal social structures within the organization. Include in this the normal decision-making patterns, informal group structures, the flexibility of employees, and what makes them tick in terms of getting the work done.
6. Identifying the preventive maintenance and repair work needed to keep the operations of your organization running, including the technology involved in the maintenance function and the tasks that must be performed.
7. Characterizing the inputs to the organization, including the suppliers and the marketing or customer environment.

The order of these steps is not particularly sacred. The logic behind beginning with a broad statement of the organization's mission and current state of affairs is that this helps to focus the remainder of the analysis on what is important to the organization as a whole. Also, the first six steps relate to the organization itself, while the seventh steps outside the organization. Identification of the inputs need not wait until the end of the analysis; they could be identified along with the outputs and major processes in the second step. The principle reason for separating these two steps is that different people may be involved in collecting the information, since knowledge of markets and suppliers and knowledge about outputs and processes will probably reside in different parts of the organization.

The remainder of this chapter will examine each of these steps in greater detail.

STEP ONE: CURRENT STATE OF THE ORGANIZATION

This step is sometimes referred to as an "initial scan." As the word "scan" implies, this is a cursory view, not an in-depth analysis of the organization. The purpose of this step is to determine the starting point of the project. Some of the items that you will want to identify are:

• Whether your redesign project will involve a new organization or a modification of an existing organization;

- The current economic situation of your organization; and
- The concern that is driving your desire for a new structure.

The questions raised by each of these topics are outlined in Figure 3–1. As we look at each area more closely, you may want to use this checklist to record your own responses.

New Organization versus Modification of an Existing Organization

An important consideration when identifying an organization's current situation is whether the organization is being designed from scratch or an existing structure is being redesigned. Most sociotechnical sys-

Figure 3–1. Current State of the Organization: Checklist for Performing an Initial Scan.

TYPE OF DESIGN

Greenfield Site
Who must become involved?
Where can they get information?

Retrofit
Will the current technology be retained or is that issue open?
What, if any, are the real constraints that you face?

ECONOMIC SITUATION

In general, what is the economic situation facing the organization?
How much time do you have?
How will the economic situation affect your available resources?

MOTIVATION FOR CHANGE

What has driven you to want to restructure your organization?
(This information may be available from your open systems planning session.)

---

tems applications fall into one of these two categories. Those that begin in brand-new organizations are typically called "greenfield" sites. Applications in existing organizations are often called "retrofits."

Greenfield Sites.   In a greenfield site, both the technology and the social system are, to a large extent, undetermined. Analysis can focus more on what should be and pay less attention to what currently exists. The advantage here is that the outcome can be guided more by your vision of the ideal. Mollifying a union—or even existing employees —is not a prime consideration: No policies, contracts, or past practices exist to be reworked or renegotiated. Working around expensive capital equipment is normally not a problem because the organization is starting with few capital encumbrances—nothing but a green field, so to speak.

Culture Considerations.   Greenfield sites are often thought to have no strong traditional culture to overcome, no history of past practices to live down, no inflexible work rules, no narrow position descriptions that make reorganization difficult. None of this historical baggage gets in the way at a greenfield site.

Well, almost none.

In the last few years, many new, small electronics companies seem to have appeared from nowhere—inspired by a single entrepreneur with an idea. The culture of each of these greenfield sites is shaped only by the assumptions and beliefs of one individual or a handful of people. Most new organizations, however, do not spring from the mind of a single entrepreneur. Start-up organizations large enough to be concerned about structure have usually been spawned by a parent organization, with its own history of past practices and procedures, an accepted technology, and a set of beliefs and assumptions that have shaped its culture. The managers and technical staff of the new organization often have come from the parent.

In these cases, never underestimate the power of the larger, sponsoring organization. "The way we did it in . . ." has a powerful influence, whether the statement is actually articulated or things are just done the way people have become used to doing them because no one questions why this should be so. Even when a greenfield organization is located far from the parent organization and barely accessible by air, the culture of the parent may seep in with the start-up crew.

If you are applying sociotechnical systems design to a completely new organization, there are fewer existing conditions for your analysis to consider, but you may still have to deal with the beliefs and assumptions that you and your staff have brought with you from old organizations. While the culture of an existing organization may not be there to hamper your new design, your own beliefs and assumptions are always with you—no matter how remotely you locate your new organization.

Employee Involvement.   A significant disadvantage of a greenfield site is that employee involvement in the analysis and design phases may not be forthcoming. The technical expertise that comes from years of doing a job simply does not exist. Most commonly, a new-location start-up has a small management crew to get it going. Many or most of these managers have had little or no hands-on experience with the work itself; their only knowledge of the operations of the organization is what is on paper. They often do not know the signals that indicate when something is going wrong. They do not know what is done informally to fix problems as they occur. This lack of experienced employees can be a drawback in a greenfield site.

Management Involvement.   The involvement of management is crucial to any organization that is intent on optimizing both its social and technical aspects. In a greenfield site, that involvement is particularly vital, because the managers usually are the only people around. However, because of the factors described above, a new-operation start-up will face special obstacles, even with management involvement. The start-up team must have a strong desire to create an effective organization and make an extra effort to understand how the organization works. Members may want to gather data from people in the parent organization, if this is practical. By interviewing those who are doing the work as it exists, they can come to understand how things really get done and what most often goes wrong. In this way, they will be less apt to duplicate a faulty system.

Retrofits.   Retrofits of existing organizations are probably more common these days than new-organization start-ups. They present slightly different challenges from the greenfield sites, the most obvious being that the existing organization is encumbered with its current practices. Existing organizations are often blinded by what *is* and may not be open to new and different options.

Constraints.   In a retrofit situation, the existing technology is often a very real constraint, because replacing it is not fiscally feasible. This means that ideal solutions may have to work around the old technology.

The current social order of the organization is also a constraint. People are accustomed to their roles and understand their relationships within the existing organization. They know what their jobs are and how to get them done—in spite of the formal system. They know how to get ahead. Often, the roles, relationships, policies, and procedures have been formalized into a collective-bargaining agreement. While union contracts are not chiseled in stone, those who have tried to negotiate changes know that sometimes they might as well be. Redesigning the organization challenges the status quo; this tends to increase the potential for resistance from all groups within the organization.

The biggest hindrance in a retrofit situation, however, is not the current organization and all its trappings—it is that the thought of these potential difficulties can become an excuse for doing nothing. The obstacles often look so insurmountable that it seems easier to live with the status quo and struggle with familiar problems than to exchange them for the unknown.

If you stand at the foot of a mountain, looking up and despairing at its height and ruggedness, you will never get to the top. You have to climb that mountain one step at a time. If organization change is the mountain you are facing, you may even find that so many others have climbed it before that they have laid down some hiking paths and you will not have to chip out a new way entirely on your own.

Advantages.   In addition to the obstacles that are probably smaller than they seem, retrofit situations have several strong advantages over the unbroken sod of a greenfield site. For instance, the problems of the current system are often well known throughout the organization, even if they are not admitted and discussed publicly. The opportunity to straighten out those snarls and snags is a powerful motivation to explore new structural possibilities. While managers may be reluctant to give up some of their perceived power, pressures from those lower in the organization counterbalance this hesitancy. If members know that the organization could perform better, that alone may provide an impetus to explore different ways of doing things. Most people would rather play on a winning team. Unless people have just given up— or unless things have gotten so bad that only those who see themselves as losers have stayed with the organization—they will probably be ready for improvements.

In a retrofit, you also have more expertise than in a greenfield situation. People who perform the work know what can go wrong and need not rely on theoretical input. Even the quality of the analysis is likely to be better, because the expertise is usually deeper than in a greenfield site.

Differing Concerns.   The most important point to remember at this stage in the analysis is that your concerns will differ according to whether you are in a greenfield site or in a retrofit situation. If you are working in a greenfield site, you need to pay additional attention to getting the kind of information that normally would be provided by the people doing the work. If you are operating in a retrofit situation, you need to be keenly aware of your organization's mission so that you are not so swamped by the constraints of the existing organization that you forget what you are trying to accomplish.

Traditional sociotechnical systems analysis does not distinguish between these two situations, generally placing equal emphasis on all aspects of the analysis in either case (Emery and Trist 1978). Most managers learn from experience, however, that the current culture of an existing organization can have a profound impact in a retrofit situation, whereas, in a greenfield site, more attention can be paid to the ideal arrangements.

Economic Situation

In Chapter 2, we discussed change as a last resort in organizations that are not economically healthy, where any action becomes better than none. If this is the point at which you are beginning your project, you should be aware of the dangers inherent in this situation.

First of all, because solutions need to happen quickly, there is little or no time for planning. While there is nothing wrong with doing an in-depth analysis quickly (in fact, there are some good reasons why the analysis should not drag on forever), the temptation is strong to abbreviate the analysis stage of the project or to eliminate it altogether. The analysis frequently becomes cursory at best. Only at this first stage of the analysis will such a cursory job, as long as it is accurate, be acceptable.

Often, the analysis will be assigned to an engineer or staff assistant to complete within a few days. While the data itself may be good, having a single person analyze the entire organization is not compatible with good results. You want to integrate the technical and social components of your organization; assigning one person to begin this integration gets it off to a rocky start. You should involve as many people as possible and give them all the time you can spare.

Another aspect of a quick scan of the economic situation may be an identification of your available resources. Is there money for an external consultant, for instance? Can a study team afford to visit other locations or even conduct meetings off site?

Motivation for Change

Very simply, this portion of the analysis is a statement of why you are doing what you are doing. What are the circumstances that have driven you to want to restructure your organization? What are the factors that are causing you enough concern that you want to invest time and human resources in improving your organization? If you and your staff or key managers have already completed a planning session, you will have this information on hand.

Articulating this motivation is important at this early stage, because it becomes part of your vision. When you tell people why you are thinking of making changes in the organization, they begin to understand where the project may lead. Most people need reasons for pursuing a project or solving a problem. This driving concern, once articulated becomes the reason, the "guiding light," for yourself, the steering group, and any others who may become involved in the project. It will become central to any communication program concerning the project.

STEP TWO: OBJECTIVES OF THE ORGANIZATION

In this portion of the analysis, you will begin building a model of your organization as an open system. In Chapter 1, we noted that the open systems model describes an organization in terms of inputs, transformation processes, outputs, and feedback. In this step, you will begin to identify some of these elements for your own organization. Feedback and inputs to the organization are covered in steps three and seven, respectively.

This analysis should be done on two levels: one for the overall organization as a single open system; and one for the elements of the organization as a series of open systems.

Overall Organization

The objectives of the overall organization should be examined in terms of the organization's mission and how that mission is achieved. Your preliminary planning session may already have produced this information. An important question to answer is, "What do our customers and clients want from us?" Another way to formulate the question is to ask, "What value do we add for our customers or clients?" Many organizations already have terms that they use to discuss their mission; there is no need to develop new jargon in most cases.

One way to clarify this question would be to identify the organization's major outputs and the core technology used to achieve these outputs. Figure 3–2 provides a guide for beginning this process.

Outputs.   Outputs may be thought of as anything the organization produces. This includes deliberate outputs as well as ancillary outputs, such as by-products or waste. (In production facilities, waste can be significant; any effort to improve the organization's effectiveness cannot overlook this waste.) Ultimately, you will probably want to work on decreasing or eliminating the undesirable outputs and improving or increasing the desirable outputs. For this reason, you must be sure to consider both at this stage. Your major emphasis, however, should be on those positive outputs produced by the organization to satisfy some demand in the marketplace or to accomplish its mission.

Transformation Process.   Most organizations use a core technology that they would identify as their major transformation process, even though they may actually use a series of transformations to turn their inputs or raw materials into outputs or products and services. A manufacturing organization, for example, may use an assembly-line technology as their major transformation process. A machine shop might describe its transformation process as "fabrication" or machining. An engineering firm may consider its major process to be designing or analysis.

If outputs can be described as what the organization produces, the transformation process can be described as what the organization does to make its products or provide its services.

Inputs.   At this point, you should also make a preliminary list of the organization's inputs—those goods, services, labor, orders, ma-

Figure 3–2. Objectives of the Organization.

___

Outputs

List everything the organization produces, including both desirable and undesirable outputs. _____

_____

_____

_____

_____

_____

_____

Transformation Process

What does the organization do primarily to manufacture its product or provide its services? _____

_____

_____

_____

_____

_____

Inputs

What resources (goods, services, labor, orders, materials, information) does the organization use? _____

_____

_____

_____

_____

_____

_____

terials, and so forth that flow into the organization to be used somewhere in the transformation process. As mentioned earlier, the analysis of the inputs themselves will be addressed in step seven, but it may be helpful to begin this list when you are thinking of the outputs and the transformation process.

Organization as a Series of Systems

A complete analysis requires that you examine each facet of the organization. The broad-brush evaluation, looking at the organization as a single model, is necessary to picture the overall approach to the organization's mission, but the trip from initial input to final output generally requires a number of transformation processes along the way.

Transformation Processes.   The simplest way to begin this task may be to list the various transformation processes that occur within the organization. This can be done by asking what happens from the time an order or request enters the system until that order or request is filled or satisfied. This analysis could take the form of a flow chart, with the output of one process frequently becoming the input for a subsequent process, as in Figure 1–2.

Direct or Supporting Processes.   Some transformation processes will be related directly to the final output. Others may be ancillary in nature, enabling steps that support the final output without actually altering the final product or service.

Accounting is an example of a support function. A customer order, an input, triggers not only the production of a product or the supply of a service but probably a series of paper transactions that account for the cost of the goods or services and ultimately produce a bill or invoice for the customer. The personnel or human-resources department may also provide support services that are designed more to cope with the environment or to shape some of the organization's inputs than to transform the output directly. The maintenance department generally provides an ancillary service that is essential to the transformation process but not a direct part of the output. Quality control and production planning also provide such services.

Distinguishing between these support services and the actual productive transformation processes will be very important as you begin to restructure your organization. Keep in mind that your goal is to make the route from input to output as effective as possible. To do that, you must be able to distinguish between what you do that serves your customer and what you do that helps you keep track of your operations. You may want to use the model in Figure 3–3 to sort out these processes.

Figure 3–3. Direct or Supporting Transformation Processes.

Based on your list of transformation processes, sort those that contribute directly to serving your customers from those that serve a supporting role only or that help you keep track of your operation.

DIRECT PROCESSES

SUPPORTING PROCESSES

*(List processes that contribute
directly to providing a
desirable output.)*

*(List processes that do not
contribute directly to an
output, such as those involved
in quality control, production
planning, training, internal
accounting, etc.)*

Concurrent, Sequential, or Interdependent Processes   Another important
distinction to make is whether transformation processes are carried out
concurrently, each being relatively independent of the others; or whether
they are carried out sequentially, each one depending on the previous
process to get started.

You may also discover transformation processes that are interdependent, that is, transformation processes that affect each other re-
ciprocally. An example might be the interaction between a traditional
quality-control department and a traditional production department.
Normal inspection tasks may begin relatively independently, but the
action that the quality-control inspector takes will depend on the
output from the production process. Rework or a new setup may be
required in the production department as a result of action taken or
information generated by the quality-control department. In other
words, the results of the production process affect the information

generated by the quality department, and the information generated by the quality department affects the ongoing production process.

Another traditional example of interdependence is the relationship between the maintenance department and most production units. Except for routine maintenance, the maintenance department's activities depend on what is happening in the production departments. When something goes wrong, the production departments become dependent on the maintenance department.

The purpose of redesigning an organization is to become more effective. In a traditional organization structure, interdependence often creates bottlenecks and delays, as well as some of the classic conflicts that consume the organization's time and energy. For this reason, interdependence or interaction between groups should be flagged during the analysis phase, because it will become extremely important during the design phase. You may want to use Figure 3–4 to categorize your transformation processes and flag those that involve any degree of interdependence.

Outputs.   Final organizational outputs have been identified in the broad-brush phase. Normally, however, each transformation process within the organization will produce an output or outputs. Some become inputs to subsequent transformation processes within the or-

Figure 3–4. Concurrent, Sequential, or Interdependent
Processes

When you have listed all your organization's transformation processes, sort them into the following categories:

1. Those that take place relatively independently of other transformation processes. (Packing renewal parts from stock, for example.)

2. Those that occur sequentially. Group together all the processes in the sequence. (The processes that occur along an assembly line or in a metal-fabrication operation are examples.)

3. Those that exist in an interdependent relationship with others. Group these interdependent processes together. (Quality control or maintenance may be examples.)

ganization; others may not (often, some reports or other paperwork fall into this category, as do waste and unwanted by-products). You may want to specify where an output is not used elsewhere in the organization or by the environment. Resources are involved in the production of any output; you may discover that some of these resources are being squandered on apparently unwanted or unnecessary outputs.

Figure 3–5 provides a convenient method for identifying questionable outputs. While reports and paperwork can be dispensed with relatively easily, waste and unwanted byproducts sometimes cannot be eliminated. However, when their disposal involves considerable expense, it may be worthwhile to consider alternate production methods that might result in less waste. At this point, all you need to do is collect the data on outputs and flag potential opportunities.

Displaying the Information

Information on the organization's transformation processes and outputs can be fairly complex—it is not the sort of data that you can convey to others orally, nor is it easily retained in the memories of those involved. Some system for organizing and displaying the data should be chosen.

Many software programs can generate flow charts that allow you to display your organization as a series of transformation processes or groups of transformation processes. The visual impact of this type of recording makes it simple to determine which transformation processes are related to each other, how they are related, and what happens to each of the outputs within the system.

Flow charts existed before the advent of the computer. A manually drawn flow chart can show the same information as a computer-generated flow chart. The disadvantage, of course, is flexibility—as more data is gathered, you must keep redrawing the chart.

Cards on a cork board can show the same information with the flexibility of a computer. However, the personal computer still has an advantage over this method in terms of portability.

One method that can be helpful for displaying, not only the flow of goods, services, and information through the organization, but also the physical geography of that flow, is a string diagram, where the layout of the existing physical facility is mounted on a cork board or other surface that will accept and hold pins. The flow of the work

Figure 3–5.   Ranking Outputs.

Once you have listed all your outputs, you may find it helpful to sort them into three broad groups, based on their importance: (1) those that are directly important to serving the customer; (2) those that are used internally to help serve the customer or improve customer service; and (3) those that belong to neither category. The outputs that fall into this third category eventually should come under additional scrutiny to determine whether they can be eliminated.

Important to Serving Customers

_____
_____
_____
_____
_____
_____
_____

Used Internally to Help Serve the Customer or Improve Service

_____
_____
_____
_____
_____
_____
_____

Neither of the Above

_____
_____
_____
_____
_____
_____
_____

and products is then diagrammed by connecting strings or threads to pins at the appropriate locations. Such a diagram is particularly helpful if you are concerned about your operation's physical layout as well as its structure. The resulting visual image can be very powerful evidence of the need for a change: In an operation where the physical changes have not kept pace with changes in the processes, the diagram is apt to look like the web of a psychotic spider.

Identifying Your Options

So far, in our discussion of identifying the objectives of the organization, we have talked mostly about analyzing the way work is done now. An important part of your analysis should be an identification of your options in reaching your objectives. Usually, any given product or service can be manufactured or supplied in more than one way. Various combinations of technology and people can achieve the same or similar outputs, with varying levels of effectiveness.

In a greenfield situation, this identification of options is especially crucial. Without the constraints of existing technology or an existing workforce, identifying the options open to you should consume more time than identifying the way work is currently done. In a retrofit situation, however, you need to step back from time to time and remind yourself that your restructuring objective is to optimize your organization, which involves generating ideal alternatives.

Throughout the process, as you collect more data or rearrange the data that you have to learn more about your organization, new and different ways of achieving your overall mission may occur to you. These new ideas are added to the data that ultimately should be analyzed before you embark on the final design.

While all the data you gather are important, tremendous potential for improvement exists in the areas you have flagged: the transformation processes that do not serve the customer directly, the transformation processes that are interdependent; the outputs that are questionable.

One way to generate more effective alternatives is to compare the organization as it currently works with the organization as it is supposed to work. A good question to ask yourself throughout the data-collection and analysis phase is, "What would the organization look like if the customer designed it?" In other words, what exactly does the customer want the organization to do, and how should it operate to get those results? Later in the analysis, we will talk more about getting information from and about the customer. For now, what you need to keep in mind is that the organization exists for some reason, to serve some purpose. Fulfilling that purpose more effectively is what the restructuring effort is all about.

You can also generate alternatives through open systems planning described in Chapter 2. Using this method, you and your staff look at where the organization is today and where you want it to be at some period in the future—five or ten years hence. The next two questions you ask are, "If we do nothing differently, where will we be at that same point in the future?" and "What must we do differently to get to our ideal future point?" These are not easy questions, but you have probably already begun asking them if you have arrived at the point where you believe you must redesign your organization.

STEP THREE: TYPICAL PROBLEMS IN THE ORGANIZATION

The third step in the analysis involves identifying what normally goes wrong in the organization's processes. What mistakes are made the most frequently? What causes products to have to be reworked? What causes service people to arrive on the scene with the wrong solutions? What activities are performed regularly to salvage other activities?

This information is often more difficult to collect than the data you have gathered so far. At this point a steering group or design team becomes very valuable; often, this information will be more readily available to them than it would be to you as the organization's manager.

Types of Information

There are three main questions that you must answer at this stage of the analysis:

* What is the problem?
* Where does it originate?
* Where is it discovered?

Nature of the Problem.   First, you must identify the problems as specifically as possible. Saying that piece A often does not fit into piece B is not enough. You need to know why the pieces do not fit. Are the sizes wrong? Are the holes out of line? Are the screw threads different? What exactly is the problem?

Likewise, the information that "the drawings are wrong" will be too vague for analysis purposes. Are they not drawn to the customer's specifications? Are the wrong drawings sent instead of the correct ones? Are drawings mislabeled or misfiled? The more specific the information, the easier it will be to track down a solution to the problem and to design an optimum organization where such problems are not likely to occur.

Origin of the Problem.   This step of the analysis must be handled with care to prevent it from becoming an exercise in finger pointing. The best way to do this is to identify the origin of the problem with a particular process or input, rather than with a person or a group of people.

For example, if you discover that part A is often slightly too big to fit into part B, you must identify and examine the fabrication processes that produce parts A and B. Something in those processes is allowing variances to occur—most of the parts are fine, but, occasionally, parts are produced that do not fit as they should. What is causing this variance? Is there a machine that does not hold its tolerances? Are there variations in the quality of the material that is used as input to the process? Is there some special fabrication technique that only very experienced operators know about?

The assumption here is that you cannot solve a problem until you know its source. If the problem occurs because of the raw material, for example, neither replacing the machine nor retraining the set-up crew or operators would be helpful. The source in that case is the supplier of the raw material, and the solution lies in that area.

Discovery of the Problem.   In organizations, problems frequently are not discovered at their source but later in the process when a misfit shows up, a quality-control inspector stops the process, or a customer complains. Sometimes, the mistake is repeated until somebody tries to use the flawed output and reports a problem.

In the optimum organization, mistakes are detected as close to their source as possible. Feedback is immediate, and corrections occur on the spot. This eliminates waste and allows early correction. For this reason, it is important to note when each mistake or problem is finally detected. The two parts that do not fit together, for example, may not be discovered until late in the assembly process, even though the variances occurred during fabrication. This is reminiscent of the difficulties experienced by the coal-mining operation described in Chapter 1, where the results that one group was expected to obtain depended on the work of another group that did not get feedback until long after they had performed their work.

Gathering the Information

Because of the rather delicate nature of gathering information about mistakes, the best approach may be to gather it from the point of discovery rather than the point of origin. Most people will be more comfortable describing all the problems they encounter when they are trying to do their jobs than they would be listing what they do that may cause problems somewhere down the line. In fact, people at the origin of the problem may not even know there is a problem.

Sources.   There are several sources of this sort of information. Quality-control reports may enumerate some of the more common problems that occur. Supervisory reports may detail some of the repeat problems. The best source of information may be employees themselves, either in individual interviews or during group brainstorming sessions. If quality circles exist at your location, minutes of their meetings may contain brainstormed lists of potential problems that could be helpful in this step. Or you could have each employee or group keep a problem log for a specified length of time. Figure 3–6 shows a sample layout of such a log.

Two important sources that fall outside the normal organizational processes are customer-service records and warranty information. These sources show what goes wrong beyond the normal processes, after the product has gone to the customer, but they should not be overlooked. Reducing your warranty costs and cutting down on the need for repair is part of optimizing your organization.

Figure 3–6.   Problem Log.

Department or Area _____

Date	Nature of the Problem	Where/How Discovered	Origin of Problem (Actual or Speculation)

Variance Matrix.   Once you have collected this information, it can be displayed in a simple matrix. Each process should have its own matrix. There are many ways to construct this table. Figure 3–7 illustrates a fairly simple approach. Along the horizontal axis of the matrix are listed all the organization's processes. In a very complex organization, if listing all the processes becomes cumbersome, you can probably list only those processes up to and including the one in question—if you are looking at problems from their point of discovery, it seems safe to assume that problems are discovered after they have been created, not before. You may also list only those problems that are revealed as significant in the problem logs.

Down the vertical axis of the matrix are listed the problems that occur frequently during the process in question. Figure 3–7 shows a typical matrix for a widget-assembly process. Some of the problems encountered in assembling a widget are that parts are missing; part A frequently is too big for part B; assembly directions are incomplete; too much oil is put in the moving joint early in assembly, and it leaks out before assembly is finished; the final step is delayed awaiting quality-control approval. The source of each of these problems is indicated by an *x* in the appropriate process column. The ideal situation would be to control these problems or variances at their source.

You will need to see the variance matrices for all processes before you begin to make decisions about rearranging the organization. (You

Figure 3–7.   Variance Table.

Transformation Process: <u>Widget Assembly</u>

Problem Sources / Problems Encountered	Purchasing	Production Planning	Machining I	Machining II	Inspection	Initial Assembly	Inspection
Parts are missing	X						
Part A too big to fit into Part B			X				
Incomplete assembly instructions		X					
Too much oil						X	
Can't finish, awaiting inspection							X

will also need the information that you will gather in subsequent steps.) If you start in one area of your operation and do the analysis only there, you are likely to miss some connections. You will find new data constantly as you expand your project, and that new data may require you to change some of the decisions you have already made. Even if you know that you are going to start your redesign project in a small way, the data collection, particularly the variance matrices, should cover the entire organization. Otherwise, you may overlook some important patterns and end up making significant changes based on inadequate information.

STEP FOUR: CHARACTERIZATION OF THE ORGANIZATION'S CULTURE

Decisions and actions are very much influenced by assumptions. As managers, we choose actions based on our predictions that they will work. Those predictions are based in large part on what we believe to be true about human and organizational behavior. All organization members are guided by their own past experiences and beliefs. The difficulty is that we often are not aware of the beliefs that enter into our decisions. Culture is typically defined as a system of shared beliefs or values, so it is particularly important to identify the shared beliefs within your organization before you begin to make changes.

Beliefs and assumptions are difficult to catalog because they are rarely articulated. In fact, sitting down cold and trying to list your assumptions and beliefs is somewhat like sitting down at the end of the day and trying to recall the number of times you blinked or cleared your throat. While not totally involuntary, assumptions are often transparent to the holder and are rarely aired unless they are questioned or challenged. Even then, the ensuing arguments may never get to the underlying beliefs.

What If?

You need some process to help uncover your assumptions. Several possibilities exist. The first is a somewhat reductive approach that involves playing "what if?" games.

Return to the list of expectations you made earlier and begin to ask "what if?" for each of them. For the second item on the list in Figure 2–1, for instance, you would ask, "What if accounting information, such as monthly billing, expenses, and income figures, were shared with the entire work force?"

The answer to that question will reflect some aspects of your organization's culture. If you and your key managers feel that the effect of such a move would be an increased potential for improvement as people understand more and more about the business, that reveals some of your assumptions about people. If you think that this action would lead to an erosion of your competitive edge because people within your organization cannot be trusted with such information, that outlook suggests a different set of assumptions.

Two basic ground rules should guide this exercise. The first is that each "what if?" should be answered with a statement, not with another question. The second is that each answer should be followed with a "why?" until you finally reach a statement or statements that reflect your basic assumptions.

As an example, look at the expectation that the organization might be able to eliminate time clocks as a method of control. We will follow that through two possible train of thought.

Example One.   What if we eliminated time clocks?

People would start coming in late and leaving early.
Why?
Because there would be no way to monitor them.
Why do they need to be monitored?
Because they don't like to work.
Why?
Because it's human nature not to like to work.

Here we arrive at an underlying assumption that people do not like to work. That assumption has, no doubt, driven many of the organization's actions up to now. Unless challenged, it will continue to be a powerful influence in the final structure.

Example Two.   What if we eliminated time clocks?

We would need another way to keep track of overtime.
Why?

Because, by law, certain groups of people must be paid for their overtime.

Why do people work overtime?

To get the work done.

Why?

Because that's what they are here for.

This questioning can take an infinite number of paths leading to as many varieties of assumptions. For instance, in the second example, the answer to "Why do people work overtime?" might have been "Because we have never been able to get the work done in the time we have allotted." This would lead to another line of questioning.

The important point is to keep asking the questions until you finally uncover some basic beliefs and assumptions that have been guiding your actions and decisions.

Fools and Rules

A second approach is described by Roger von Oech (1983) in his book, *A Whack on the Side of the Head*. He calls it "The Fools and the Rules" approach. Basically, it involves analyzing a rule or procedure in the role of a devil's advocate or naive fool. While you may not talk yourself out of the rule or procedure, you may uncover some interesting arguments against it that cause you to question some of your assumptions.

Again, a look at the items in Figure 2–1 or your own list of expectations might serve as a point of departure. Taking the second item in Figure 2–1, for example, we might state it as a rule: Accounting information, such as monthly billings, expenses, and income figures, should be shared with the entire work force.

The fool's role is then to rebut that rule with arguments as wild or controversial as possible. For example: Accounting information should not be shared, because then people have no idea where they stand and can always believe that they are doing well. If they believe that they are doing well, they will be much more eager to come to work, and they won't feel nearly as much stress. They will be able to relax when the going gets rough. They won't feel the need always to improve and beat last month's figures. We may actually save medical benefits for stress-related illnesses if people are kept in the dark about our financial progress. After all, ignorance is bliss.

While this approach does not reach underlying assumptions as directly as "what if?," it can begin to challenge much traditional thinking.

Use of a Consultant

Both of these approaches are difficult to do on your own, even with help from others within your organization. In fact, if you want to use a consultant for only one step of your analysis, this step may buy you the most value. You can use a consultant to facilitate the "what if?" or "Fools and Rules" exercises, or you can let the consultant apply his or her own techniques for helping you uncover assumptions.

The advantage of using a consultant here is that an outsider can question the reasons of an organization more naturally than an insider can. Entering a strange organization, an outsider often sees and questions practices and beliefs that an insider does not recognize. Some of the practices that a consultant might question may be irrelevant; for example, an observation that managers' and hourly employees' paychecks are different colors may or may not be significant. The point is that an insider probably would never question such a practice, while an outsider would notice it and be curious.

Another reason for using a consultant may be the nature of your organization's culture. People may be more willing to talk to an outsider than to an insider. A person who is outside the normal power structure of the organization may seem like a neutral, safe conduit for relaying information.

The consultant can help you build a picture, not only of the assumptions and beliefs held by those within your organization, but of what it is like to work in your organization in general. A consultant may use individual interviews, group interviews, or other techniques to create this picture of what it is like to work in your organization and why.

This picture will be useful for several reasons. First, it will give you a benchmark from which to launch your organizational change. Once you have designed and described your optimum organization, you can compare that vision with your existing organization, so that you know where to begin the change effort.

Second, the data will give you an indication of how easy or difficult it will be to effect a change. If people believe that the way they are currently doing business is the only way to go, then your change effort must begin by educating them to see other options. If, on the other hand, they show a willingness to try other techniques or strategies, they will be more open to change and may even exert positive pressure to build the new structure.

Third, the data will help pinpoint where current assumptions are congruent with the future direction of the organization and how widely held they are.

STEP FIVE: CURRENT SOCIAL STRUCTURES

Like step four, step five involves looking at the social or people side of your organization. Specifically, step five is intended to identify what people do to make the organization work: typical decisionmaking patterns, informal group structures, the flexibility of employees, how work normally gets done, and employee motivation.

Typical Decisionmaking Patterns

Traditionally, organization structures are depicted on a chart showing reporting relationships. The formal organization chart can be the starting point for an analysis of decisionmaking patterns. List the decisions that occur at each block on the chart—not in theory, but in actual practice. Distinguishing between the decisions you would like to have made at a particular level in the organization and those that actually are made there is very important at this point: Often, because the organization is designed to have decisions made at a certain level, we assume that those decisions occur there, when, in fact, they do not.

An example is the decisions made by a first-level supervisor, particularly in a production facility. We usually ascribe to that person decisions about administering discipline, while in actual fact, first-level supervisors often feel that they have little control over these decisions because they must clear them with their managers, as well as with the personnel department. When decisions require approval by higher levels, you must question whether they are being made by those who originate them or by those who approve them.

Budget decisions are also often misleading. If budgets for one level are drawn up by a higher level with little room for variation, then the first level, which appears to be responsible for budget decisions, really is not; those decisions are actually made at the level above: The reverse could also be true. A budget for an upper level may be assembled and monitored by the level below, with the apparently responsible level serving only as a repository.

Sometimes, decisions that seem logically to be made in one area are actually made by default somewhere else. For example, in the absence of a strong marketing presence, a clerk on the loading dock may be deciding which customers' orders are shipped and when.

Figure 3–8 provides a convenient form for collecting this data. After completing this analysis, you will know which decisions are being made by whom, which will allow you to determine whether you are satisfied with the current pattern of decisionmaking. The analysis further distinguishes between recommending actions, making decisions, approving action, and implementing the final decision. This categorizing is essential: Ultimately, if you want your organization to be more responsive to changing customer needs or market demands, you will need decisions to be made as close to the level of implementation as possible.

Accurate information on decisionmaking is crucial. You can encourage this precision by letting everyone in the organization know how important this accuracy is to you personally and to the success of the organization in general. To ensure that people do not try to protect you from unwelcome surprises, you should make it clear that there will be no penalties—real or perceived—for such information. Any negative responses on your part or on the part of those collecting the data will tend to cause people to shape information into what they think you want to hear. People must feel free to describe decisionmaking as it really happens—not as they think you would like it to be.

Informal Group Structures

Just as decisions are not always made as the organization chart suggests, so the informal organization chart does not always look like its formal counterpart. You need to identify that informal organization.

In most traditional organizations, there is a certain amount of interdependence between departments or functions. Manufacturing relies on engineering for drawings; engineering needs feedback from manufacturing about producibility—the feasibility of manufacturing a particular design. Marketing needs output from manufacturing, and

Figure 3–8. Typical Decisionmaking Patterns.

Brief Description of Decision	Who Recommends Action?	Who Makes Decision?	Who Approves Action?	Who Implements Decision?

manufacturing needs orders from marketing. Because these functions rely on each other to various extents, people normally develop some relationships across functional lines. Informal task groups may spring up to get work done. Certain people are identified as those to turn to for information about their particular functions. As a result, these people gain informal power within the organization. Networks develop around them. You will even find informal structures within formal divisions. Natural leaders spring up.

Frequently, these informal structures and methods of operation can be described fairly accurately. Simply asking people how they get things done and to whom they talk may uncover this information. First-line supervisors may possess more of this data than anyone else, because they have become masters at getting work done through the informal channels. They generally know who has the information they need and how they can go about getting it.

The secret to getting good information in this area is the guarantee of impunity. You may not like what you learn, but you must not punish those who inform you.

Flexibility of Employees

If you are striving for a more flexible organization, you need to determine the existing level of flexibility. In particular, you need to know how broad your employees are in terms of the skills they currently possess or the variety of work they are capable of performing.

Often, information about skills is already available in personnel records. Sometimes, just studying the job histories of your employees will give you an indication of the breadth and depth of their skills.

How Work Normally Gets Done

The description of how work actually gets done in your organization may be the most eye-opening piece of data that you collect. In fact, how far the actual process diverges from the prescribed process is some indication of the need for a new organization structure. If you discover that work is getting done exactly as you would expect it to be done based on the written policies and the formal organization chart, your structure may be in fairly good shape. But if you find that what actually happens bears only remote resemblance to what should happen, then you can be certain that your decision to redesign your organization is sound.

The data will also give you some idea of what it takes to make things happen in your organization. You should pay special attention to the informal relationships revealed by this information: Who talks to whom to get things done? Which departments constantly must check with each other? How much time is spent in this double checking? Keep in mind that your optimum organization will allow work to be done in the most effective manner possible. The informal organization will become formalized or legitimized so that it can work efficiently and effectively.

Often, first-line supervisors can tell you what people *really* do to get work done. In one very old organization where I supervised a group of white-collar workers, I discovered quickly that the best way to find out what was happening was to talk to the clerks. They knew who talked to whom and exactly what transpired to get both products and services out to the customer. I sometimes thought that if all the managers left for a month, most of the work of the organization would have gone on without missing a beat.

Figure 3–9 lists some of the questions that you might ask to find out both how work gets done and how the informal organization works.

Employee Motivation

The final piece of data that falls into this general social category is the motivational drive of your employees. Generally, it is helpful to know what makes your employees want to work. Are they simply there for a paycheck? Do they work to support a hobby? Do they enjoy fixing things? Do they like to make decisions and be in charge? Do

Figure 3–9. How Does Work Get Done?

Who meets with whom? Why?

When the normal procedure doesn't work, what happens? Who initiates this action?

How do you find how something has gone wrong?

How do you find out about changes in priorities?

Who has the most accurate unofficial information? Where do they get it? How do they disseminate it?

When you need something from another department, to whom do you talk? Who actually gets you what you need?

they like turning out good work? Just thinking through what different people have invested in your organization may help you reach conclusions about their level of motivation.

Sometimes, your managers can take fairly accurate guesses at what motivates the people with whom they work. They usually have already identified those who enjoy doing good work and those who get their kicks outside of work. However, when you gather data this way, you need to be sure that your managers' assumptions do not color the data too much. Managers who tell you, for instance, that none of their people enjoys doing good work may be revealing their own beliefs about why people work rather than the actual motivation of their employees.

Information about employee motivation is important for at least two reasons. First, you want to avoid designing an organization that requires people to become more involved in the work than they want to be. My own opinion is that you will always find a few people who will not be happy with being more involved in their work because they are saving their involvement for activities outside the job. But you will also find plenty of people who have been waiting for the opportunity to have a job that they can really care about.

Second, the discovery that most of your employees strongly want your organization to be successful offers tremendous encouragement to you as the leader initiating change to improve the chances for success. Some managers have not given much thought to how their employees feel about the organization's success. Others may assume that employees have little interest in the long-term success of the enterprise.

Years ago, when I was transferred into a very old manufacturing plant, I discovered an interest in the long-term success of the organization that I had not expected to find. While employees may not be as highly motivated to make the organization succeed as are entrepreneurs themselves, in this case, they were certainly more concerned about the long-term success of the business than those of us who were transferred in and out as part of our career development. Our focus was much more on making short-term improvements that would reflect our own promotability than on what we might do to effect more long-term gains. The employees, on the other hand, had an enormous stake in the business's fortunes—they had no place else to work nor any desire to leave the organization.

STEP SIX: MAINTENANCE NEEDED

This step deals with the technical side of your organization and looks at what kind of maintenance—both preventive and corrective—is necessary to keep your equipment running. One of the decisions you must make in designing your new organization is how to handle these maintenance tasks.

In the optimum organization, where you have eliminated as much interdependence between departments as possible by integrating support activities into production activities, maintenance presents a special problem. Do you leave it as a separate support function? Do you build it into the production function? Do you change the way that you reward the function?

Before you can begin to answer these questions, you need to know what is involved in the maintenance of your facility. Perhaps one of the easiest ways to collect this information is by the following two-step process. (You may want to use the form in Figure 3–10 to record your data.)

First, list all the equipment used in a process that requires maintenance. Generally, this includes everything with moving parts that you normally repair rather than replace—typewriters, word processors, lathes, presses, rolling mills, robots, and so forth. It may also encompass electrical, electronic, hydraulic, pneumatic, and mechanical equipment.

Next, list all the maintenance, preventive and corrective, required to keep the equipment running smoothly. This can include everything

Figure 3-10.   Maintenance Needed.

Process _____

Equipment Used	Brief Description of Maintenance Needed	Preventive?	Corrective?	Skill and Technology Required

from regular cleaning and simple adjustments to complex trouble-shooting and overhauling. Particularly important to note is the maintenance currently performed in-house.

You also need to mention the technology and skill involved in the maintenance. The skill and technology required to oil a machine periodically, for instance, is much different from that required to calibrate delicate instruments or to determine why a piece of equipment will not work.

All of this information will be valuable when you are making your final design decisions. If you are striving for flexibility and quick response, you will want to minimize the amount of downtime you experience while people are waiting for limited maintenance resources to make minor repairs or adjustments to their equipment. You may want to build the maintenance capabilities into certain groups to improve both their quality and their productivity.

STEP SEVEN: INPUTS TO THE ORGANIZATION

So far, you have looked only briefly at the inputs to your organization. This step is best conducted by the people who are most knowledgeable about the organization's inputs. The purchasing department probably knows most about the suppliers, and the marketing department probably knows most about the customers.

Suppliers

American business has begun to learn from the Japanese the advantages of more cooperative relationships with their suppliers, and you may already have sufficient data in this area and a solid working relationship with your suppliers. If so, you are ahead in the game.

Just-in-time inventory techniques are beyond the scope of this book, but they are perfectly congruent with a sociotechnical systems design, which requires close working relationships with suppliers. One of the reasons that these relationships become so important is that, throughout the organization, you are going to be trying to control problems at their source. This means that you should not be performing quality control for your suppliers; this should be their job. You should be getting what you have specified and paid for—and you should not have to verify that such is the case.

If you have not already developed these relationships, the first step is to identify who your suppliers are and what they supply. You will also need to discover what problems are associated with incoming goods and services. To some extent, an open system works according to the old computer adage, "garbage in, garbage out." If problems in inputs are not corrected ahead of time, you may not get garbage at the other end, but you will have to modify your processes considerably, provide special treatment or handling, and generally expend extra resources to get good outputs from poor inputs.

Your purchasing people may have much of this data, but your production people will probably have quite a bit to add as well. Figure 3–11 illustrates one form that production people might use to collect this data. They know best which of the materials they receive are good and which cause them problems. Using a cross-functional team for data collection in this area will probably get the best results.

Marketing Environment and Customers

If your organization is to have any longevity at all, you need to know what customers want today as well as what they are apt to demand tomorrow. You need to know what the marketplace is doing and what the marketplace is expected to do in the future. These data will help you identify appropriate outputs, as well as the degree of flexibility that you will need to produce them.

Figure 3–11.   Inputs to the Organization: Supplier Data.

Material Used	Problems Encountered	Special Treatment or Handling Required	Current Supplier

Your marketing experts should be good sources for this information. If some of your employees deal directly with customers, they, too, will be excellent sources of information. They may receive comments from customers, for instance, that the marketeers never hear. Service representatives frequently respond to complaints that never reach the sales representatives' ears, because sales people often are not around when a product breaks.

If you are going to view your organization as an open system, interacting with its environment, you must be able to characterize that environment accurately. You must know what to expect from your environment. And you must know what your customers expect from you. Only when you know what your customers really want can you design an organization to meet their needs.

CONCLUSION

The data-collection phase can take as much or as little time as you desire. If you are starting slowly, you may want to spend more time in data collection just to accustom people to the idea of change. If you want to spend as little time as possible, much of the data can be gathered concurrently. In many ways, time and resources are interchangeable during this phase: Many people can collect data simultaneously, or a few people can collect it piece by piece.

My own inclination would be to condense the process, using as many people as possible. Not only does this allow you to gather more accurate data, but you also get more people involved in the process and, at the same time, demonstrate a greater commitment on your part. The project tends to pick up momentum during the analysis phase, rather than losing it as data collection drags on and on.

When you have gathered all of this data, you are ready to begin interpreting it to discover your optimum organization.

4 DESIGNING YOUR ORGANIZATION

Alternatives, and particularly desirable alternatives, grow only on imaginary trees.

—Saul Bellow, *Dangling Man*, 1944

After you have completed your data collection, you will have a lot of information about how your organization works and a greater understanding of where improvements can be made but few concrete answers about the organization's ideal structure. Information alone does not give answers. You—and your staff, steering group, or task force— must analyze it, asking questions and making connections to create an overall picture. You need to arrange the data so that it forms that broad picture, showing the kinds of relationships that currently exist among functions to keep the organization running. You also need to understand how members feel about the organization and how willing they are to make changes. Only then can you begin to develop alternative structures and select the one that is most appropriate for your business.

The decisions that you must make concern what you will use as the basic building blocks of the organization and how you will hold them together. "Building block" questions concern whether you will structure the organization around individuals or groups.

"Glue" questions deal with the kinds of relationships or interdependencies you will select within and between the pieces of your organization. To the possible consternation of some construction experts, we will look first at the glue and then turn our attention to the building blocks. Understanding the relationships between units makes designing the units somewhat easier. In addition, focusing first on the relationships places the emphasis on the organization's *results*. You must be able to achieve these results to keep your organization competitive.

SELECTING THE GLUE

Organizational structures are characterized by the nature of the units that they comprise and the nature of the relationships among those units. One of the key pieces of information that you have gathered shows the relationships between various functions within the organization. Both the open systems model of your organization and the variance tables that you have generated reveal the current inter- and intragroup relationships in your organization. To some extent, your technology influences these relationships. But several different types of relationships or interdependencies can exist. Understanding the nature of these relationships is critical to the final design of the organization.

In most cases, you will discover that the existing interdependencies often have dictated both your structure and the kinds of issues that you must manage. As managers, we often do not realize that we can control these interdependencies. However, to a very great degree, your organization can be designed to feature the kinds of interdependencies that you prefer so that you can focus on the issues that you believe are important.

Determining the Relationships You Have

Three types of interdependencies are cited most often to define the relationships among the units or tasks in an organization (Thompson 1967). Units may be individuals or groups of individuals. The simplest relationship between units is usually described as "pooled": various units or tasks operating fairly independently, coordinated through rules and procedures. Units that are linked in some sequence have "sequential" relationships: One unit must perform a task before the next unit can begin its task. Finally, "reciprocal" relationships refer to the most complex form of interdependency, in which various units

Figure 4-1. Pooled Relationships.

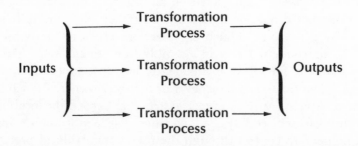

must adjust their responses mutually, based on what is happening at any given time.

Pooled Relationships. Especially if your organization deals with services, rather than products, your open systems model may not be an orderly chain of inputs, transformations, and outputs, linked together one after the other; instead, it may have a number of very short, unconnected input-transformation-output chains, as in Figure 4–1. Banks, savings-and-loan associations, and many fast-food outlets are examples of organizations that typically experience these kinds of disconnected relationships.

Perhaps these are often termed pooled relationships because every transaction is treated similarly, regardless of the customer. The inputs to the organization are all pooled together, awaiting a transformation that will release them from the system. When I go to a bank, I do not need to see the same teller that I saw the time before, nor do I need to withdraw the exact amount of money that I put in the last time. In fact, once I deposit cash, it is very unlikely that I will ever again see the same currency with the same serial numbers as the cash I deposited previously. As long as the banking institution uses the same rules to process my account that it uses to process anybody else's account, I care little which currency is issued to me.

Some fast-food restaurants also operate, at least partially, in a pooled relationship. The inputs to the customer-service area are dozens of "MacWhoppers," stored in a warming area, which will be sold to all customers that ask for them. Any burger will suffice for any customer, because there is little or no differentiation within a given product group.

Typical Structure.   If depicted on an organization chart, organizations with pooled relationships will have either "flat" or "tall" structures. Any given part of such organizations tends to be flatter than would be its counterpart in an assembly-line organization. The fast-food restaurant, for instance, frequently has shift supervisors, whose efforts are coordinated by a manager or manager-owner. Branch banks are also relatively flat. However, the structure beyond the local branch or the single franchisee may be much taller. The height stems primarily from the need to control through the use of standardized procedures and rules; often, many layers of management are considered necessary to monitor both the creation and implementation of these procedures and rules.

Rules and procedures are very important in these organizations. For example, I would be upset if I found out that my banking institution paid another customer twice the interest that I received for the same size of deposit over the same length of time; or that one of the tellers always multiplied my deposits by two, while another recorded only half of what I deposited; or that, at the end of the business day, the tellers got together to determine the day's most pleasant and most unpleasant customers and to transfer funds from the latter to the former.

Key Issues.   In an organization with pooled dependencies, management attention generally focuses on controlling adherence to rules and policies. Often, even the dress of its members is mandated by organization. The thrust is toward conformity.

Because conformity is fairly easy to gauge, pooled relationships are perhaps the simplest to manage. Organizations with these relationships are designed to be flexible only within narrowly defined limits. Managers often have little more discretionary power than those under their control. Increasing the flexibility of an organization based on pooled relationships means changes the very nature of the organization in many cases.

Sequential Relationships.   Perhaps your open systems model takes the form of a neat flow chart, with one transformation process feeding output into the next until a product or service emerges from the final process. (See Figure 1–2.) This relationship is often referred to as sequential, since processes occur in a sequence. Assembly-line operations are a typical example of sequential relationships between processes. Each person at a given station needs to perform his or her task before the product can move on to the next station.

Typical Structure.   Sequential relationships do not permit a particularly flexible structure. Improving productivity generally means trying to shorten cycle time, either by reducing the time spent at each station or by performing several groups of tasks simultaneously (with these subassemblies coming together at a certain point), which breaks the long flow of processes into several shorter flows.

While shorter legs may reduce cycle time, they tend to complicate coordination. Generally, each feeder leg or subassembly area is a separate department with its own manager or supervisor. Since these supervisors need to coordinate their efforts, managers are usually appointed over groups of them, with several of these group managers reporting to a manufacturing manager. Manufacturing must be coordinated with purchasing, production planning, and quality control, so an operations manager often is appointed to supply that coordination and control. Finally, operations, engineering, and marketing must be coordinated, so still another level of management must oversee the entire organization, including the ancillary functions that were created simply to measure and monitor the line functions.

Key Issues.   Managing work in a sequential flow requires a great deal of planning, because each operation in the sequence must be ready with the appropriate skills, tools, and materials when the product or service arrives at that point in the process.

The assumption in many organizations with sequential relationships is that if everyone does his or her part, the final outcome will be okay. As a result, most management effort is directed toward getting people to behave in certain ways to keep up their part of the process. Measurements tend to focus on individual cycle time, attendance, and inventory.

Absence and tardiness frequently become the critical human-resource issues that managers try to control, because they create gaps in the sequence. Emphasis is often placed on starting and quitting at the specified time, because late starts and early quits tend to have a domino effect in a sequential operation. Control measures include time cards and check-in procedures. Quality control generally becomes a checking function in organizations of this type.

Unfortunately, none of these measures have much at all to do with customer satisfaction or quality results. Often, very little is said about the customer in these organizations; measurement systems receive more serious attention. We may say that the customer comes first and the customer is always right, but few organization members ever see the customer, and most of them understand time cards and productivity measurements much better.

Reciprocal Relationships. If the open systems model of your organization showed feedback running back and forth between transformation processes and initiating new transformation processes, then you are probably dealing with reciprocal relationships. (See Figure 1 −3.) Many service organizations have these kinds of internal relationships. Often, the customer is the nexus of all the relationships, and the organization must make continual readjustments in order to provide service that meets customer needs.

A hospital emergency room is a typical example of an organization with reciprocal relationships. Doctors, nurses, and technicians working on a patient in an emergency room constantly are receiving feedback both from the patient's condition and from each other. This feedback modifies what each person is doing.

Research-and-development organizations also frequently have reciprocal relationships where breakthroughs or failures at any point in the process require adjustments throughout the system. Repair operations may themselves involve reciprocal relationships—often, not until a service representative visits the customer does the organization know what kinds of skills, tools, and technology must be applied to the problem at hand.

Typical Structure. In successful organizations with reciprocal interdependencies, structures tend to be relatively flat, with decisionmaking occuring at the interface with the customer or client. Because responses must meet changing conditions, there normally is not time for bureaucratic decisionmaking procedures. While a hospital may develop an administrative hierarchy that might resemble that of an organization with sequential relationships, the power of individual doctors is largely unchallenged in most medical procedures. A more traditional structure that cannot accommodate reciprocal relationships often frustrates medical personnel.

Many organizations with reciprocal interdependencies have evolved from more traditional organizations and are still struggling with the changes they must make. Often, organizations that need a great deal of flexibility or whose various units have become integrated because of new manufacturing technology or the demands of competition must work with structures more appropriate to simpler types of interdependencies.

In organizations with reciprocal relationships, managing through rules and regulations is overly cumbersome. Centralized decisionmaking is disastrous. People have to understand the processes well enough to be able to do whatever it takes to reach an appropriate outcome.

Key Issues. Generally, in organizations with reciprocal relationships, the focus is on assuring that members understand the organization's goals and have the appropriate skills to reach them. Results, as measured by the customer, are what count. Emphasis on attendance or written procedures is noticeably out of place in these organizations and adds little to the bottom-line results. A familiar event in the hospital emergency room is a good example. While the doctors, nurses, and technicians on a trauma team are ready to spring into action at a moment's notice to do whatever must be done to save a patient, the clerk at the admitting desk often adheres rigidly to hospital policy, stubbornly collecting demographic and insurance information from the patient or whomever has accompanied the patient. While this makes amusing material for comedians, it contributes little to customer satisfaction and may actually detract from the final results in the emergency room. But admitting clerks work for the part of the organization that is structured around pooled relationships; their job is to collect the same information from each patient, based on a written policy or standard.

Determining the Relationships You Want

The data you have collected will help you to identify the interdependencies within your own organization. You may discover that your entire organization can be characterized by a single type of relationship or that different areas of your organization have different relationships. In a manufacturing plant, for instance, the renewal parts department frequently represents a pooled interdependency—extra parts are stocked in some standardized fashion and shipped to anyone who orders them using their standard part numbers. The manufacturing process, however, may involve sequential relationships, with each section or department adding to the sequence until a finished product emerges. If the product requires considerable installation or service work at a customer's site, portions of the organization may operate with reciprocal relationships, in which field service representatives do whatever it takes to make the final product work or to keep the customer satisfied. If your organization has all three relationships and you have been trying to manage them all the same way, you may already have received some feedback that techniques that work for one do not work for another.

Focusing Your Management Efforts.   A critical question that you must answer at this point is "What kind of interdependencies do you want?" Or perhaps even more appropriately, "What do you want to spend your time and efforts managing?" Your focus is determined to a large extent by the types of relationships in your organization. Figure 4–2 lists some management priorities and their relation to the three interdependencies.

Focusing on Standards.   We have already mentioned that the key issue in organizations with pooled interdependencies is adherence to rules and policies. Standards are set to control behavior, and those standards must be maintained. Management efforts are frequently aimed at making sure that reports are filled out properly, dress codes maintained, and transactions handled precisely the same. While some results are reported and tracked in these organizations, those obtained through methods outside the narrow, accepted channels are frowned upon.

Figure 4–2.   What Do You Want to Spend Your Time Managing?

Management Focus	People Issues	Type of Interdependency
Standards	Conformity	Pooled
Planning and control	Absenteeism and tardiness	Sequential
Results and direction	Skills and commitment to goals	Reciprocal

However, this approach is not the only path to success. In organizations in the same industry with the same technology, you often will find some managed as though the relationships are pooled and others managed as though the relationships are more reciprocal. Airlines are an example here. In some airlines, a flight attendant on a sparsely passengered flight who distributes the extra bags of nuts may be asked to account for the missing snacks. In others, flight attendants will go out of their way to provide little "extras" to passengers, particularly on flights that are not crowded.

Another example is the fast-food industry, which began, as we have described, with organizations that treated their customer relationships primarily as pooled. Then some fast-food chains began differentiating their products by treating their customers more individually. You could ask for certain variations in the product, and your request would by-pass the pool to be made separately. Still others began assembling their products to your specification *after* you ordered. In these cases, an entire shift crew behind the scenes had to respond to each individual customer's order.

Pooled interdependencies generally create more predictable organizations than do reciprocal interdependencies. There is nothing wrong with predictability; in some parts of some organizations, it is very important. Where that is the case, pooled relationships are probably best. However, where predictability is a handicap, as it may be in a highly turbulent environment where flexibility is needed or where customers demand more individualized service, pooled relationships may be inappropriate. The choice is yours.

Focusing on Control. We have already mentioned that sequential relationships require considerable planning efforts to ensure that the process flows smoothly and that all people are on the job and doing their jobs right. Control is the watchword of the sequentially structured organization. Production control, quality control, and inventory control are discussed frequently and often even merit their own departments and managers. Time clocks or time cards, production clerks, and quality-control inspectors are the glue that holds sequential relationships together. Absentee rates, work-in-process, net-allowed hours, finished-goods inventories, overages, shortages, and rejection rates all are intended to confirm whether the controls are working.

If you want to focus your efforts on control, you should probably select a sequential relationship for your design.

Focusing on Results.   In an organization designed around reciprocal relationships, the focus is on making sure that every employee understands the organization's goals and has the skills and knowledge necessary to achieve those goals. While this seems fairly straightforward and, intuitively, a logical approach to managing an organization, we have not been living with pooled-relationship and sequential-relationship structures for decades only because managers have ignored the obvious until recently: Those relationships are *simpler* than reciprocal relationships; they are often easier to manage, or perceived to be so, and are probably easier to staff. Before we faced stiff foreign competition, before rapidly changing technology forced us to become increasingly more flexible, before customers became so demanding, these simple structures were quite adequate—our world was a simpler place. Unfortunately, that era is waning rapidly. The good news is that, as necessity has forced us to examine our assumptions and our old ways of doing things, we have discovered that reciprocal relationships can be structured to be managed more easily than we once thought possible.

Determining the Placement of Relationships.   While reciprocal relationships at certain levels of the organization can be the key to remaining flexible and competitive, they can be disastrous at other levels. The important point is to understand how these relationships work at various levels and how they can become liabilities instead of assets.

Current Placement of Relationships.   Your overall systems model of the organization will help you identify what kinds of relationships you have now, where they are, and how they work, but some hidden features may be found in your variance tables and problem logs. Any log or table showing that most of the problems found in one unit or process originate in another unit or process is evidence of some reciprocal interdependency. When a problem detected in unit A, can be traced back to unit B, you know that unit A depends on unit B for performance and unit B depends on unit A for feedback. If the two units are widely separated from each other, that relationship can be a problem. The product or service tends to bounce back and forth between these units until the output of one is a suitable input for the other—or until a higher authority intervenes to settle the matter.

This situation is not uncommon. In organizations with many sequential relationships between units, the product of one unit frequently becomes the input for a subsequent unit. Where work is designed so that the first unit only receives feedback after its product causes problems later on down the line, there are often serious delays. Recall the discussion in Chapter 1 of the productivity drops that occurred in English coal mines when each shift became dependent on the previous shift.

The problems become even more serious when the relationships are more reciprocal. Consider a game of checkers, which places two people in a reciprocal relationship with each other. The decisions that one makes are dependent on the plays that the other makes. In this face-to-face relationship, reciprocity presents no real problems. However, if the two players are no longer the decisionmakers, the relationship becomes cumbersome. Before each player can make a move, he must first describe to his boss the situation on the playing board and his opponent's last play; perhaps, in turn, she must relay this information to her boss in order to get a decision. A simple game of checkers becomes a lengthy, complicated mess.

A similar phenomenon occurs in organizations when reciprocal relationships exist between units that are organizationally separate. If the decisionmaking authority resides at the same level where the several units mutually must adjust their actions, as when two people playing checkers decide and make their own moves, problems are few. However, if units that must accommodate each other's actions must refer to a different level in the organization for permission or directions, considerable delays result. If the marketplace demands quick response and flexibility, the health of the entire organization is threatened.

Your open systems model tells you what kinds of relationships exist in your organization by showing how the units are linked. Examining those linkages carefully, especially in light of the variance tables, and problem logs can help you to identify which relationships are working well and which are causing problems. This information is essential in creating new design alternatives.

Strategic Placement of Relationships. We have established that you need not retain the relationships that you already have but can select the kinds of relationships that you want to manage, based on your overall vision of your restructured organization. We have also observed that you may have several types of interdependencies within your organization, which depend on the nature of the tasks and the nature of the customers. The next critical step is to determine how to combine the interdependencies to create your optimum organization.

In a nutshell, the most effective arrangement is to keep reciprocal relationships within units and pooled relationships between units. Where sequential relationships slow down the operation or require considerable planning and control overhead to manage, consider changing them to reciprocal or pooled relationships. These guidelines are simple and hardly immutable, but they may help you get the maximum benefit from the various kinds of interdependencies.

Reciprocal within/pooled between.   Again, checkers illustrate fairly easily the reasoning behind this arrangement. Remember that the relationship between two opponents in a game of checkers is reciprocal. That relationship works quite well as long as they both control all the resources they need, including the power to make decisions about which pieces to move. If someone else must supply them either with decisions on what to do or with the equipment that they need to begin the game, the process is slowed down.

Imagine now a checkers tournament, at which many pairs of players compete. Each pair represents a reciprocal relationship. The relationship between pairs, however, is pooled during the tournament: Each pair is governed by the same rules and procedures, but there is no need for interaction between pairs.

If we examine an automobile assembly plant in which teams of employees assemble complete cars, we see a similar arrangement. The relationships within teams are reciprocal, but, between teams, the relationships are pooled. Each team works toward the same goal, using the same drawings for any given model that they assemble. Each team probably is not quite as autonomous as a pair of checkers players, because it may have to depend on other groups or individuals for materials.

In the last few years, managers have read about "loose-tight" connections in organizations (Peters and Waterman 1982). The argument is that leaders manage some areas tightly and others loosely, and the trick to good leadership is knowing the difference. The same concept can apply to organizational structure. Ideally, you want to divide your organization at its natural breaks, where the relationships within any unit are "tight," while the relationships between units can be "loose." This is achieved best when intraunit relationships are reciprocal and interunit relationships are pooled.

No sequential. So far, we have said little about where sequential relationships fit into the design. More and more in today's organizations and marketplaces, sequential relationships are becoming obsolete, luxuries that we can no longer afford. For the most part, we cannot move quickly enough to stay ahead of the competition if we have to take one step at a time. Automobile manufacturers that used to employ sequential relationships in their design processes have discovered that these structures are too slow. When a marketing group conducts a study and hands the results to a design group, which then designs a product and hands the result to a manufacturing group, which then must build the product for sale to dealers, the entire process takes years.

Sequential structure generally does not work as smoothly in practice as it does on paper. In fact, the handoff from one group to another, particularly from design to production, is often referred to as the "grenade-over-the-wall" approach. In nearly all cases, this method cannot compete with foreign manufacturers, which have reduced the time from concept to completion to a fraction of ours. Indeed, when we have to produce quickly, we often use the informal organization of the "skunk works" to get things done. Generally, in these cases, work is accomplished through continuous mutual adjustment, rather than one step at a time. A new product team is created, which includes marketing, design, and production expertise. Questions are answered and problems solved as the project proceeds, rather than at the end of each step, when the ensuing resistance and political infighting often debilitate the organization. In other words, reciprocal structures are adopted temporarily to meet a crisis.

As we have noted, both pooled relationships and sequential relationships require simpler structures than reciprocal relationships. For many years, in fact, I advocated remaining with the simpler structures whenever possible. However, our world has become too complex, our technology is changing too rapidly, and our competition is emerging at too great a rate for our simple, well-understood structures to succeed. Quite simply, the bureaucracies required to manage pooled and sequential relationships no longer work in today's environment. It is time to move on to more complex relationships.

Yet, although the relationships themselves may become more complex, the organizations may actually become simpler. Consider again our checkers players. In a room full of checker-playing pairs, little coordination is required to keep them all playing. On the other hand, if the players have not been empowered to make moves without asking for directions, the task of coordination becomes nightmarish.

SELECTING THE BUILDING BLOCKS

What do we mean by the building blocks of the organization? A standard organization chart provides a good preliminary illustration. If the lines on the chart represent the relationships (pooled, sequential, or reciprocal) between the boxes on the chart, then the boxes themselves represent the basic building blocks. These building blocks (or units) can be either individuals or groups. Unfortunately, just as you cannot tell what kinds of relationships exist between units by looking at the lines on the chart, you also cannot usually tell what the building blocks are by studying the boxes on the chart.

To identify your current building blocks, you must look more closely at policies and procedures, and especially at reward systems. How are salaries and wages determined? Are people paid for their individual performance or for overall group results and their contributions to those results? What sort of behavior is rewarded? Are people encouraged to pitch in and solve problems to get results, or are they rewarded for "keeping their noses clean"? Do informal groups spring up to make the system work? Conversely, do informal groups work against the system? Or are formal groups in place to get the work done? Are exhortations such as "be a team player" indicative of a real condition of employment? Or are they merely rhetoric?

Figure 4–3 contrasts some of the characteristics of individuals and groups as building blocks. While other differences may also be identified, these are some of the key characteristics that define the two sets of building blocks. When individuals are rewarded for individual performance, informal groups work to get around the system (for either positive or negative results), and team playing is only rhetoric, the building blocks are individuals. In organizations where individuals are rewarded for their contribution to a group, "being a team player" is an actual condition of employment, and formal groups are in place to get the work done, the building blocks are groups.

The primary question you must answer is whether your optimum organization should be built around individuals or around groups. Some of the decisions you have made concerning the relationships that

Figure 4–3. Building Blocks of an Organization.

Individuals	Groups
Compensation level determined strictly by individual skills or knowledge.	Compensation level determined by value of the individual's skill or knowledge to the group.
Rewards accrue to individuals and are allocated based on individual performance.	Rewards accrue to groups and are allocated based on individual contribution to the group.
Individuals are accountable to a boss.	Individuals are accountable to a team, which may then be accountable to a boss.
Coordination is provided by individuals or departments whose chief job is to coordinate activities.	Coordination within the group is the responsibility of the group. The need for coordination between groups is minimal, provided by a manager whose chief job is "boundary management."
Special problems may call for the formation of problem-solving groups or task forces that are not part of the formal structure.	Most problems can be solved within the normal structure of the organization.
"Being a team player" is usually just a phrase heard in pep talks.	"Being a team player" is a condition of employment.
Organization units tend to be grouped by function and composed of people with similar jobs or families of skills.	Organization units tend to be grouped by tasks and composed of people with the variety of skills needed to complete an entire project.

you want to manage will point you in the direction of the units that are appropriate for accomplishing your mission, but variations are possible.

Individuals as the Units of the Organization

Individuals in a Pooled Organization.   If you have discovered that your organization is best held together by pooled relationships at all levels, your structure may be best composed with individuals as the chief building blocks. In these cases, the relationship between the customer and the organization members may be either pooled or reciprocal, but there is little interdependence among individuals within the organization.

An example of such an organization is a law firm that handles cases of a routine nature. Lawyers performing relatively simple services for clients who may or may not establish long-term ties with the firm will operate fairly autonomously. The individual cases bear little or no relationship to each other. Clients come in with routine requests for unrelated services; they may see the same attorney each time they bring in a new case or problem, or they may work with different attorneys on different matters. There is little or no need to coordinate efforts between firm members; instead, emphasis is placed on regulating the efforts of individual members through adherence to legal and ethical codes. Efforts are also coordinated through some common fee structure and billing system. Individual lawyers may be paid based on their current case loads, or they may simply draw a salary. In either case, their individual compensation is based on their own merit and does not depend on the performance of others. Lawyer A has little need to know what Lawyer B is doing.

Under these circumstances, the individual is clearly the building block of the organization. If this arrangement is working, there is probably little reason to change it. However, if we look at an organization with similar technology but a different client base, we might see potential differences. In the same law firm, suppose the clients began reporting more complex problems or wanted to develop long-term relationships so that the firm could handle all of their legal problems. In either case, it might no longer be possible for individuals to operate independently. Lawyers might have to work together to provide several types of expertise to solve a complex legal problem or a variety of long-term services to a single client.

In this case, the building block of the organization may become groups of lawyers, rather than individuals operating independently. Results, from the clients' point of view, are not based on the performance of a single individual but on the work of the group of experts that handles their work.

Individuals in a Sequential Organization.   While individual structures may be ideal in pooled organizations, they are also often found in sequential organizations, where they may be less appropriate. In these cases, where individuals operate in a string of operations, each dependent on the previous one for input, the entire sequence moves only as fast as the slowest individual.

This individually based sequential structure and the phenomenon of the slowest individual as pacesetter were the catalyst for the principles developed by Frederick Taylor. In a sense, scientific management tried to re-create the advantages of a pooled relationship within a sequential operation, dividing work to the point where operations were so quick and so simple that the slowest individual was no longer a problem.

While scientific management methods seem to have solved this problem, other problems are created when the environment demands flexibility or when new technology creates the need for greater skill.

Individuals in a Reciprocal Organization.   As we have already described, when individuals must adjust their actions mutually to work closely with each other, the structure becomes more complex. Normally, in these organizations, individuals tend to function in groups, because they must work so closely together.

The emergency-room trauma team is an example. People with varied skills and levels of expertise work as a single unit to save the lives of critically injured patients. They act by responding to each other and to the patient, as well as by drawing on their own skill and knowledge.

The difficulty in structuring such an operation around individuals, rather than around their membership in the trauma team, stems from divided allegiances and differing sets of rules and standards. If the nurses, for instance, report to a nursing supervisor for guidance; the orderlies report to an orderly supervisor for guidance; and the doctors report to a chief resident, and so on, the trauma team may never become a high performance team. Individual structures tend to work against results in an organization that requires reciprocal relationships.

Advantages of Individual Structure.   As we have pointed out, structuring an organization using individuals as the building blocks is generally less complex than using groups as the primary unit. Where relationships between individuals are pooled, this lack of complexity provides a real advantage.

One reason why we may think that structures built around individuals are simpler is that we are more familiar with such organizations. Most of the compensation systems we see are designed to reward individual performance, rather than group performance. We understand better how to measure individual performance. We are better equipped to coach and counsel individuals. We also know how to recruit and hire for individually structured jobs. Most of us cannot claim such familiarity with group-based compensation, measurement, performance management, or selection procedures.

Disadvantages of Individual Structure.   If relationships are reciprocal, structuring an organization using individuals as the units creates coordination problems. If I must work with you and adjust my actions to match yours so that we can achieve certain results together, then I want to know how the organization is going to measure and reward what we are doing. Who gets credit for the outcome? If I help you, will you get the credit for the results? What will the organization see as my results? What kind of recognition do my efforts get? I also want some assurance that my manager is going to let me work with you and that someone will not pull me off to do "my own" work every time you and I begin to work well together.

We see that the typical problem is one of accountability or responsibility. In these cases, the group building block achieves better results.

We have already mentioned that tremendous coordination is required to keep tasks moving at an acceptable pace, rather than at the pace of the slowest individual, in organizations with sequential relationships between individuals. Overhead in the form of planning and control functions diminishes the competitive advantage of these individually based structures.

Groups as the Units of the Organization

Organizations are always composed of individuals but need not be structured around them. Where relationships between tasks tend to be more reciprocal than pooled, groups probably make more effective building blocks than do individuals.

If you have already looked at the relationships that would be most effective in your organization and read the preceding discussion of individuals as building blocks, the chances are that you have already begun to draw some conclusions about whether groups would be appropriate units in your organization. At this point, the best approach may be to reinforce your conclusions with some observations about the conditions that are best suited to group structures and a summary of some of the key issues that you will face in structuring an organization around groups.

Conditions Suited to Groups.   J. Richard Hackman (1977) has described four situations in which group-based designs are probably more appropriate than individually based structures. First he believes that groups are more appropriate when a high degree of interdependence is required to get work done. We have already discussed this situation at length and reached a similar conclusion.

Hackman adds three other conditions, however, which are worth discussing further. Groups, he says, are more appropriate as building blocks when meaningful individual work is not possible, when individuals have strong social needs, and when the motivating potential is higher in a group. All three of these conditions are closely related to the issue of motivation.

Only Group Designs Will Yield Meaningful Work.   Most management consultants and behavioral scientists will probably agree that people are more highly motivated to perform work when that work is meaningful to them. This holds true at all levels, and you yourself can probably think of several tasks that you consider meaningless and find difficult to perform with any great relish.

While different people find meaning in different types of work, several generalizations are probably true. Meaningful work usually involves a whole task (as opposed to a piece of a larger task), some degree of variety, and a feeling that what is being done has some significance to the final outcome of the organization (Hackman and Oldham 1980).

If you accept these parameters, many jobs, especially in sequential relationships, lose their meaning. If I tighten a few bolts and pass the work on to you, and you do the same, neither of us will find much meaning in our jobs. Although we may be highly motivated to perform our current management jobs, we might become demotivated very quickly under these circumstances.

Often, a group design will allow people to work together to build an entire product or perform a complete service, solve problems as they go, and see the results of their work in the finished product or satisfied customer.

Individuals Have Strong Social Needs.   If you have learned over the years that the people in your organization have strong social needs, then you may leverage that impulse by designing an organization with groups as the basic unit.

One indication that the people in your organization have a strong need to socialize with others may be that when you walk through their work areas, you find them clustered in groups, talking. Another might be that even insignificant events have a way of triggering a party or a pot-luck lunch. Spending time with each other after work is also an indication that people are attempting to form themselves into groups. Groups tend to form in many organizations, even informally, just to get the work done. In organizations where there is strong emphasis on individual behavior, however, this informal grouping becomes a problem—the result may be a less-than-optimum outcome.

Groups Provide Greater Potential for Motivation.   Finally, in terms of the motivational potential of a group versus an individual structure, you need only consider the stories you have heard or the events you have witnessed in which "rate busters" were handled by the group whose rate they busted. In these cases, the motivation of the group *not* to produce was stronger than the motivation for additional income or the urging of the supervisor to produce more.

Imagine the potential of the group if its goals were aligned with the organization's mission. While, quality-control inspectors cannot build quality into a product and first-line supervisors cannot mandate either productivity or quality, a high-performance team on a roll is a formidable force to deal with from your competitors' point of view. Group pressure to perform well can be as powerful as group pressure to prevent rate busting. The secret is to harness that potential.

Key Issues in Structuring Around Groups.   One of the most important questions to answer in structuring an organization around groups is, "Who goes into what group?" In other words, how do you decide what groups are appropriate and who should belong to each group? Where do you draw the lines separating one group from another?

The best answer to these questions is another question: What makes sense? We will look at what makes sense from two perspectives. First, we will consider what makes a "whole" group. Second, we will discuss how various arrangements would affect the relationships or interdependencies both within and between the groups that we create. Both of these issues are related.

Wholeness. In organizational structure, the term "wholeness" does not refer to some new-age mental-health craze, but rather to the old ideas of responsibility and accountability. Ideally, when we say that a group should be responsible for a whole task, we mean that the group should have the responsibility for seeing that the task is done, the accountability for doing it right, and the resources to see the task through. A whole task incorporates feedback so that the group knows when its work has been completed correctly. If a group has a whole task, no one else should have to point out mistakes or problems: The work itself will do that, and members will be able to correct errors and solve problems before their product or service leaves their group.

The game of bowling is an excellent metaphor for the wholeness concept. People like to bowl because they can see the results of their efforts, work to improve their results, and get encouragement from those around them. Imagine what would happen to the enthusiasm of a four-person team if a heavy soundproof curtain were hung about halfway down the alley, and two players rolled balls, while the other two counted knockdowns. Imagine, too, that the second team has been told that its job is to reset all the pins as quickly as possible after each round. This "job description" will certainly affect the quality of the feedback transmitted to the ball-rolling teams, since it is hardly in the interests of the pin-setting team to have too many pins fall down. Its members may even begin to give positive reinforcement for gutter balls, because then they can accomplish their task in the least possible time.

This analogy sounds ludicrous—no one would ever behave this way in a bowling alley. But before you scoff too loudly, think about the organization that you yourself have known. Often, the quality-control department gets rewarded for finding errors, not for helping the production department correct them. The order department takes information from customers but may not even be part of the feedback loop when a customer complains that an order was filled incorrectly.

Steven Kerr (1975) pointed out that we often reward people for one activity but hope for another. In the bowling example, for instance, the pin setters are rewarded for speed in resetting, but it is *hoped* that they will also give good feedback to the ball rollers, so that the overall score will improve. This problem is not so much a question of misplaced rewards as it is of poor structure. No one person or team is totally responsible for the outcome of the game. Each aspect is measured and rewarded separately, but no one is measured based on the whole game, except maybe the person who is overseeing it. We are right back in Chapter 1's English coal mines. People are doing what they are rewarded for doing, and often they are doing that very well. The problem is that the manager or owner may be the only one who is being rewarded for the final total outcome.

A standard bowling arrangement, with an entire four-person team trying to knock down more pins than the other four-person teams makes much more sense in terms of the wholeness criterion. Each team is responsible for its outcome, receives immediate feedback on how well it is doing, and sees some meaning in the process. Even if players have to take time out to run down the alley and reset their own pins, these teams will probably make more progress than the teams in the divided structure.

Attention to Relationships Between Groups. Because games have been devised to be fun and to have champions, any organization structure that violated the rules of good game design by tampering with interdependencies or relationships would probably be suspect. Again, this may be a particularly helpful comparison, because the nature of all groups is to compete with each other. In bowling, competition between teams improves the quality of the league. Even though only one team wins, the other teams improve their skills and their outcomes by competing. Overall, the league chalks up points as the teams vie to become the best. The league coordinator wins over other league coordinators.

The secret to using this game analogy is to be careful about what sort of game you pick when you are designing your structure. If you have teams playing against each other in a Monopoly design, for instance, keep in mind that only one team will win and the other may wind up bankrupt in the process. Playing against a big winner in Monopoly, you do not necessarily get better, but you do get poorer in terms of resources. The same would be true of two teams competing against each other in a checkers match: One team will have to lose resources for the other to win.

This is often the situation in an organization where the interdependencies are between teams and not within teams. Remember our simple relationship rule: reciprocal within/pooled between. New product design is a good illustration of this rule.

When a new product must be introduced, the kind of competition and the overall result depend on the structure of the organization. If a marketing team, a design team, and a production team are formed separately and a deadline is set for product introduction, there is a Monopoly-type result. Marketing does its best job on the front end with surveys and data. The design team may find the customer requirements impossible to fulfill but does the best job it can and is careful to dot all the i's and cross all the t's in preparing the perfect design. The production team may find the design unproduceable and has little time left to produce it. But, by that time, the outcome is

Figure 4–4. Checklist for the Design of a Work Group.

Does the Group Have a "Whole" Task?

Is the group responsible for getting the task done, or does that responsibility lie with someone else?

Is the group accountable for doing the task right, or does it pass the work on to another person or group that will uncover errors?

Is the group able to allocate its own resources (time, budget, etc.), or does it have to rely on another source to allocate resources?

Does the performance of the task itself provide the group with feedback, or must it wait until someone else discovers whether the work was done right?

How Does the Group Relate to Other Groups?

What effect does the success of this group have on the success of other groups?

Can one group's success spoil the results for other groups?

Does competition between groups cause them all to be better and the organization to become better at the same time?

---

probably moot, because the competition may already have introduced a new product and cornered the market.

A different design would have one team working on a particular new product line and another team working on another new product line. It really doesn't matter which is better. As long as they both get there before the competitor, they will both win. In this structure, the team members represent marketing, design, and production and can adjust their actions and their thinking as they go to reach the best outcome for the marketplace.

Figure 4–4 provides a checklist for structuring a work group according to the principle of reciprocal relationships within the group and pooled relationships between groups. These questions may provide useful guidelines in the formation of your own work groups. All of the questions should be answered for each unit of your proposed structure.

SUMMARY

Aided by the guidelines and information regarding relationships and building blocks provided in this chapter and using the information that you have collected for your own organization, you and your staff, steering group, or design team will work out the design of your new structure. For each unit in each design alternative that you generate, you could ask the following questions.

1. What are the relationships of the people within this unit?
    A. Will they work independently of each other (pooled)?
    B. Will each of them have to complete a piece of work and then pass it on (sequential)?
        i.   If so, how will the pace of the slowest individual affect your ability to be competitive?
    C. Will they have to work closely with each other to adjust mutually what they are doing (reciprocal)?
        i.   If so, will they have all the appropriate skills and resources to be able to see when adjustment is necessary?
2. What are the relationships between this unit and others?
    A. Does this unit depend on any other unit for information or resources to start its work?

      i.   If so, how much control does it have over the quality of that information or those resources?

     ii.   What sort of feedback loop is in place back to the sources of the information or resources?

3.   Is this unit designed so that it can control its own quality, or does it depend on feedback from other units about its work?

   A.   If the latter, how does feedback reach the unit?

      i.   Does it come in time for the unit to adjust its work to avoid repeating the problem?

     ii.   Is the information about its performance meaningful and understandable?

The answers to these questions will tell you what kind of relationships you have both within each unit and between the units. The variance tables that you drew up in the last phase will help you with the feedback information, which is critical when looking at relationships between units. If you find that units are still very dependent on each other for resources and feedback, you may want to rethink the structure. You may not be able to eliminate interdependence between the units, but you need to be sure that the relationships make sense.

For the most part, designing a new structure is an iterative process. Each alternative should be subjected to rigorous scrutiny. Each time you think you have the right structure, draw an open systems model of it and create variance tables to see what kinds of relationships exist between the units.

The ultimate question to ask is whether your new structure will allow you to perform better than your competition. In the end, that single criterion is the ultimate measure of performance.

5 IMPLEMENTING THE NEW STRUCTURE

There is a time for departure even when there's no certain place to go.
—Tennessee Williams, *Camino Real*, 1953

When you take your first step from the old to the new as the manager responsible for actual implementation, you will probably feel as though you are jumping off a high dive. In a first dive, the fear really does not go away until you are finally in the water, and then your chief concern becomes staying afloat. The lesson to remember is that, before you take your first dive, you had better know how to swim.

Such is the case with organizational changes. Continuing to study the situation will not allay the fears. But, before you implement your new structure, you should understand what you can expect and how your organization is going to operate under the new system.

With that in mind, we will consider some of the issues you need to look at before you leap and some of the strategies and techniques for taking that first plunge.

IMPLEMENTATION CONSIDERATIONS

The prime considerations for actual implementation are "How much?" and "How fast?" More specifically, how much of the new structure do you want to implement at the outset and how quickly will you move to change the entire organization? There is no single correct strategy, but reviewing the advantages and disadvantages of the various options will help to develop a tactic that is best for your own circumstances.

Vision

Whether you begin by restructuring one part of the organization or the entire organization, whether you move quickly or slowly, one critical component of your implementation will be your vision of the final outcome. A clear vision of the entire structure is essential so that the rest of the organization can see what the new structure will look like and how they will fit into the whole.

Integration.   Your vision of the whole is especially crucial if you decide to work with only a piece of the organization at a time. In this situation, the people who are beginning to function under the new structure and the new rules must realize that they are the model for the entire organization, not just guinea pigs in an isolated experiment. People who are in parts of the organization that have not yet changed must be able to look at what is happening in the newly changed areas and understand that they, too, will soon be operating under the same conditions.

Expectations.   Knowing what the future truly holds is not nearly as terrifying in most cases as conjuring up ill-informed images of what might be. A clear vision will help everyone in your organization understand better what is expected of them and what they need to do to move in the new direction. The vision of the new structure will strengthen further the overall organization's mission and direction.

Basis for Feedback.   Another advantage of articulating the vision of the new structure at this point is that you and your steering group or design team can get feedback about whether the new structure is working. If no one knows what the final structure is supposed to be, they cannot be expected to provide helpful feedback about whether or not the changes are working. Entire pieces of the organization can get off to a false start and head in the wrong direction. But if they understand what the outcome is supposed to be, they can continually measure their own progress and behavior against that vision to judge whether they are moving in the right direction.

Direction.   When people understand the nature and purpose of the new structure, they can spot difficulties and report them in such a way that you can modify design details to eliminate the problems. With a clear vision, these modifications appear like simple course adjustments to reach a desired outcome. Without a clear vision, however, even minor modifications appear like directional changes. Organization members become confused and frustrated. Sometimes, they begin to doubt their own abilities; more often, they begin to doubt yours.

An Analogy.   A sailing analogy may be helpful here. A good sailor can take a vessel to any destination, although, depending on the direction of the wind, it may not be as the crow flies. When sailing against the wind, the sailor must tack back and forth at angles to the wind to reach a destination. People who have never been on a sailboat before often are not aware of this. If you fail to tell them how a sailboat works and where you are going, they probably will not be able to guess from watching the helmsman steer. The person at the helm gets no credit for well-executed tacks if the crew does not understand the method or the destination. They may simply believe that the helmsman is lost.

The same is true in an organization. When you begin making changes, people need to know where you are headed and what the guiding principles are for reaching your goal. They must understand that you may not be able to go there directly and that you may have to adjust for shifts in the environment or even for early miscalculations, much as a sailor may have to adjust for sideslips or wind changes.

If the organization does not understand your vision, you may find some members hiding below decks, rowing at cross-purposes, or throwing out anchors every time they reach a spot that appeals to them. You cannot expect people to help you reach your destination if they have no idea what that destination is or what kinds of tactics you are planning to use to get there.

Whole or Part

Study and design should encompass the entire organization so that relationships and work flow can be seen clearly. Performing the study and design piecemeal may leave you in no better shape than you were before you began. You need to study how all the pieces fit together in order to identify the relationships and find the optimum design. But you need not *implement* all the changes at once. You can change your entire organization all at once or gradually, piece by piece.

Scope of the Change.   One factor that may influence your decision is the scope of the change you are introducing, in terms of both the degree of difference between the old and the new and the size of your organization.

Difference between Old and New.   If the new units and relationships are very different from the old ones, it will be more difficult to make changes in one part of the organization at a time. You cannot simply isolate an existing section and begin changing the way it operates; you must form new sections, taking people from existing sections to do so. If this is your situation, you may want to implement incrementally across the board, moving to some interim structure. Sometimes, you can move people into their new positions but introduce them gradually to new ways of operating. Another option is to move a few people into the new structure and let them begin working in new ways and then extend the changes to the rest of the organization.

To illustrate how a gradual approach might work, even if the change is fairly dramatic, we will look once more at an organization that is trying to introduce new products as fast as, or faster than, its competitors. If this is a large organization with a traditional functionally based structure where marketing, engineering, and production are separate departments, it might be best to begin the change gradually by forming one or two teams to develop and produce new product, moving a few people from the traditional structure into the new structure, without dismantling the entire organization. If everyone knows that this is the first step toward the new organization, they will understand that this is not a temporary task force in which the members retain their allegience to their functional managers. In this way, the change is "piloted" before it is introduced across the board. (We will discuss "pilots" in more detail later.) However, at some point the final pieces of the organization will have to be drawn in to the new structure all at once.

Size of the Organization.   In a small organization with less than 100 people, there is probably little need to implement structural changes bit by bit. In large organizations of more than 500 people, implementing the changes all at once will be more difficult and may prove to be impossible. Between these extremes, the area is gray. Here, the nature of the change may be your guide.

Even if the change itself is not drastic, the sheer size of a very large organization limits your ability to implement any change all at once. But you may be able to make the changes in one area of the organization at a time, particularly if areas are physically separated from each other, and each can be treated as a separate organization for implementation purposes. However, your vision should be clearly and widely articulated so that everyone, even in areas that are not currently affected, knows what to expect.

Other Considerations.   If you are moving from an organization that uses individuals as the critical unit to a structure with teams or groups as the key unit, many supporting changes must be made throughout the organization. We have already alluded to the need for different reward systems. New ways of managing, new ways of thinking about training, and new ways of solving problems, perhaps even new ways of selecting people, are also necessary. These changes are the subject of Chapter 6. They need not all be implemented at once, but the organization must know that you are aware of the need for the changes and that you and your steering group or staff will ensure that the new structure receives all supporting changes necessary to make it a successful, competitive organization.

Starting with a Pilot.   If we think for a moment about the word "pilot," the role of a pilot project in a change implementation will become apparent. A pilot steers a vessel to its destination, making course adjustments to account for variances in wind and weather. The role of a pilot effort in an organizational change project is similar.

Advantages of a Pilot.   Perhaps the greatest advantage of a pilot implementation is that mistakes can be contained, examined, and learned from. In a sense, piloting the new structure in one part of the organization is like diving off the low board before trying the high dive. You still have to have thought the process through and you still have to know how to swim when you hit the water, but you can perfect your diving technique under less demanding conditions. By working first with a small piece of your organization, you can use the results there to make adjustments in subsequent segments. Even if you plan to implement your new structure all at once, you may want to consider a pilot in a part of the organization before you implement the change officially across the entire system.

Often, the pilot can create a desire for change in the rest of the organization, particularly if it is combined with a clear vision of the ultimate organization. When others see what is being achieved in the pilot area, they often want to be a part of that success.

A pilot also allows time for the rest of the organization to prepare more gradually for change. The other members can practice their swimming strokes, so to speak, while they watch the pilot group perfect its technique on low dive.

Choosing a Pilot Group.   You would not want just anybody piloting an aircraft in which you are a passenger; neither do you want to pilot your new structure just anywhere in the organization. You should choose your pilot area carefully, with an eye toward maximum success. You do not want the rest of the organization to watch someone belly flop into shallow water; you want it to witness a successful dive.

One of the characteristics of a high-potential pilot group is that the participants are interested in change and motivated to make the new structure a success. If there are people in your organization who believe that the new structure will diminish their power or influence, they are not appropriate candidates for inclusion in the pilot.

You also should not select an area whose task or mission has a low probability for success. For example, if your design involves moving part of your organization from functionally separate departments to product or customer-based departments, you should not designate as your pilot group the department with the most difficult product or least stable customer.

You also want to be able to learn from any less-than-optimum outcomes, so that subsequent changes can be more on target. For this reason, you want to start in the area that will be the most "forgiving" in terms of overall business.

The pilot area should also be relatively visible to the rest of the organization. If the pilot becomes a raving success but no one else witnesses the improvement, you will have lost the opportunity to generate enthusiasm in the rest of the organization.

Ideally, your pilot area should be fairly independent from the rest of the organization. Input and feedback have a powerful influence on a group's success. The group should exercise some control over its

Figure 5–1.   Checklist for Locating a Successful Pilot Area.

Good Choice

_____	People involved are interested in change.
_____	People involved are motivated to make the organization successful.
_____	Product involved is sound.
_____	Customers involved are solid.
_____	Pilot is visible to the rest of the organization.
_____	Pilot area is relatively independent from the rest of the organization.

Poor Choice

_____	Many people in the pilot believe that the new structure will limit or reduce the power or influence they hold currently.
_____	Product involved is at or near the end of its life cycle.
_____	Customers involved are on the brink of taking their business elsewhere.
_____	Pilot group is dependent on other areas in order to do its work successfully.

---

input and receive feedback from its own work. If it is too dependent on groups or individuals within the old organization for input and feedback, it may not have enough control over its performance to achieve success. If others in the organization are extremely resistant to the change, the doomsayers may throw a wrench in the pilot's works. They may deflate the pilot group's performance simply by withholding feedback.

Figure 5–1 provides a convenient checklist of the characteristics that distinguish a potentially successful pilot area from one that is potentially harmful.

Rate of Change

Change has three speeds that concern you in the implementation phase: too fast, too slow, and just right. Like Goldilocks wandering through the deserted house of the Three Bears, your job is to choose what is "just right" for your own organization. Some guidelines may help.

Too Fast.   As we have already discussed, if your organization is large and the changes are fairly dramatic, an all-at-once approach may be too fast. A good rule of thumb is that any change that moves too quickly for people to understand what is happening is too fast.

It is important to remember that, by the time you and your staff or steering group have come to the point of designing a new organization structure, you feel practically intimate with the impending changes. Unfortunately, most of the people in your organization will not have been as deeply involved, although many of them should have participated in some of the data gathering, at least. But, in most organizations, the entire work force cannot get involved in organization design all at once; most will need some time to absorb your vision and to understand the reasons behind the changes and their roles in the new organization. Several iterations of the information are likely to be necessary before everyone understands. Some people will need to observe actual change before they will understand completely what is happening.

You also need to be sure that your rate of implementation allows you time to adjust the details of the change as you go. The supporting policies and procedures, especially, will take some time to get right. As many managers remind themselves in these days of turbulent change, "You have to eat an elephant one bite at a time." Any attempts to engorge will produce only indigestion.

In an early sociotechnical systems restructuring with which I was involved, the organization was small, and we were able to move quite quickly, incorporating a tremendous amount of work-force involvement even in the planning stages. In fact, we moved so quickly that at one point we had to slow things down—the management members did not yet understand their new roles and what behaviors were expected from them and needed a chance to catch up. This kind of speed is not always possible or prudent. If you are moving from an individually based structure to a group-based structure, you may have to allow more time for people to learn how to work together in groups and for managers to learn how to facilitate groups. If you new units require more flexibility, you may also have to allow more time for training.

Too Slow.   For most people, moving too fast is an easier problem to understand than moving too slow. Yet, managers are often cautious by nature, and we may be more in danger of moving too slowly than the reverse.

While training and understanding have plenty of time to catch up in a change effort that is moving slowly, other problems plague creeping change efforts. The biggest danger is that the organization operates for too long with mixed signals and people become confused. Parts of the organization operate under old rules, while others operate under new rules. Often, some rules have been altered to facilitate the change, but others remain intact, their revision delayed until its nature becomes apparent. Some people are rewarded for one type of behavior; others are rewarded for the opposite behavior; still others are reinforced randomly for either type of behavior.

It becomes obvious why organization members often perceive a lack of commitment on the part of management when change efforts move too slowly. In a gradual implementation, you can have your cake and eat it, too, for only so long. There comes a time when you must begin to move everything in the new direction.

Just Right.   For any organization, there is a rate of implementation that will reap both the benefits of a slow, gradual introduction and those of a faster, full-bore changeover. No formula exists to calculate the perfect speed, but neither is there anything sacred about the speed at which you begin. If you start off your implementation too fast, you can slow it down; if you move too slowly, you can speed up. Listen to what people in the organization are saying and watch what is happening. This feedback will serve as a speedometer. Reading the signals from the organization so that the rate of introduction can be adjusted will be an invaluable service that your steering group can perform.

If you discover early on that many people understand neither the change nor their part in it, you may have to slow down until you can do some more communication or training. If you hear rumblings that management is not really committed to this "experiment," you may want to speed up the implementation and focus more effort on supporting the change. As long as people understand the overall vision and why you appear at various times to be tacking or hauling sail, you are free to make adjustments without impairing your success.

TAKING THE PLUNGE

The watchword in implementation is *congruence*. Ultimately, in a so-ciotechnical systems approach, congruence means that the people and the technology will work together in harmony. In the early stages of implementation, however, the chief focus is the harmonious relation-ship between the actions being taken and the overall vision for the project.

As we discussed earlier, what you and your managers do from the announcement of the change through the implementation can help or hinder your chances for overall success. The entire organization will watch you for clues as to what the changes mean. Many may search for evidence that the changes are an aberration and that things will return to normal soon. They, especially, will look for evidence that you are not serious about your vision. If your own actions do not model the behavior that you want from the people in your organization, you send everyone a signal that nothing will really change. "This, too, shall pass" becomes their motto.

What's in a Name?

As trivial as it may seem, what you do or don't call your change effort can be a factor in its success and acceptance. A pilot, particularly, is often referred to as an "experiment," which suggests that the change effort may not really be serious. After all, some may reason, if an experiment fails, it will hardly be implemented throughout the organization.

If such is the assumption in your organization and if people are suspicious of the experiment, the chances for success probably decrease in inverse proportion to the number of people hoping for failure. Admittedly, this is more of an intuitive axiom than a proven theorem, but, nonetheless, the use of the term "experiment" generally should be avoided in an organizational change effort.

Some managers have reported that calling the change anything but a change encourages people to think that it may be just another "program of the month." Titles that end in "program" or "project" seem to give people the idea that this is something that they can do and be finished with, rather than a new way of working or a new way of doing business. If you find it convenient to tag your vision with a simple moniker that can serve as a rallying point, be sure that the name indicates that the changes are leading to a new way of life within the organization.

Search for Inconsistencies

One question that you might want to display prominently in your office is, "What would I do right now if the new organization were fully installed?" The sooner you begin to behave as you will in the new structure, the sooner you will send clear, consistent messages to the people in your organization. Your vision will seem much more real if you back it up with consistent behavior on your part.

The most important training that you can give your managers early in the process is an understanding of their roles and behavior in the new organization structure. They, too, will be under scrutiny for signs of inconsistency or some evidence that they are not really committed to the changes. Some people will be looking for indications that the old way of doing things is here to stay; others will be looking for proof that management never did know what it was doing: Neither reason is helpful to the organization. The last thing you need at this point is for people to be pulling in different directions.

CONCLUSION

The best way to implement your new structure is in the manner in which you hope to run the improved organization. The actions that you and your managers take during implementation will be observed closely. If they are not congruent with the vision that you have communicated, people may conclude that you do not take your own vision seriously. Such a response will make it difficult for you to gain their commitment to the change effort.

Whether you start with a segment of the organization, whether you move quickly or slowly, the most important factors in implementation are consistency in the actions that you take and widespread understanding of the direction and vision. Your own actions and decisions must support the new direction and the new structure. But, beyond that, people must have a clear understanding of where you are headed, so that they do not misinterpret directional corrections as inconsistencies that indicate a lack of commitment on your part.

With a clear understanding by the members of the organization and a strong commitment from you and your management team, your organization will be launched solidly toward optimization.

6 SUPPORTING THE NEW STRUCTURE

You cannot drive straight on a twisting lane.

—Russian Proverb

We introduced the subject of sociotechnical systems by describing it as an approach that allows you to link people and technology optimally. This linkage, we said, represents a whole system of connections within the organization: connections between the social aspects of the organization and the technical aspects of the organization, connections between procedures and final results, connections between the way that you structure your organization and the issues that you choose to manage. When you complete the analysis of your current organization, these connections become more apparent. As you begin implementing your new organization structure, they become more important than ever, because you cannot succeed without supporting the new configuration with changes throughout the organization.

The policies and procedures that you used to support the work in your old organization may not suit the new structure. They may not support the new behaviors that you are trying to nurture. If people become committed to your vision, you may not even need many of the policies with which you maintained control in your old structure (Walton 1986).

Reward systems, both formal and informal, may also need to be changed. If you have been rewarding people for individual performance and are now operating in a group-based structure, your reward system must support that change.

123

Because many organization members will be playing different roles, training will be needed in order to support those new roles and behaviors.

You may even need to think about how you will select people for your newly designed organization. You may have to involve teams in selecting their own members and to screen for ability to work in groups, as well as for skills and experience.

In a single chapter of a single book, we cannot hope to cover all the contingencies that might fit your particular organizational change. Instead, we will concentrate on these four areas, where changes must be considered to support a move from a structure using individuals as the building blocks to a structure using teams or groups as the building blocks. This change is common in organizations adopting a sociotechnical systems approach. It is also perhaps the most dramatic change you can make and, as such, requires some of the most drastic changes in your support systems. If you restructure your organization but continue to use individuals as the building blocks, the changes will be not quite so dramatic, and the supporting systems may need only adjustments, instead of changes.

REWARD SYSTEMS

In the optimum organization, reward systems must connect the individual's performance to the performance of the enterprise as a whole. You want everybody working toward the same overall goals, and you want the reward systems to support only positive efforts towards those goals.

Despite the apparent simplicity of this dictum, many organizations wind up rewarding intermediate goals that may not always be conducive to their overall performance. This was a problem, you will recall, in the English coal mines. Those who drilled holes for blasting, for instance, were rewarded for the number of holes they drilled, although the mine owners hoped that they would also drill them right so that blasting and extraction could proceed without too much difficulty. Another example that may hit closer to home is the practice of rewarding employees for attendance. There is nothing wrong with this practice, but it is driven by the unspoken assumption, or hope, that when people are on the job, they are actually doing productive work, moving the organization toward its goal. Such an assumption may or may not be justified.

Managers from manufacturing organizations may be familiar with the perpetual quality/quantity dilemma, which is particularly conspicuous near the end of a billing period. We tend to reward people for getting the product shipped, no matter what its condition may be; meanwhile, we talk about quality and *hope* that we ship a quality product. Traditionally, we have not rewarded whistle blowers who complain about the quality of the outgoing product and about having to ship something that is not up to the standards that we profess to want.

In my early days as a supervisor in a section that fed subassemblies to a final assembly line, I heard constant complaints from the final assembly people about how they were told to ship. In those days, the company rewarded people for two things: being on the job and building a product that could be boxed for shipment. Most of the workers had never held jobs in industry before and they began by assuming that they would be rewarded for building a quality product. Over the years, we almost managed to convince them that they should be rewarded for good attendance and putting together a product that could be boxed. When we finally wised up, we managers had some unlearning to do. We had to learn, for instance, that our orders to "ship it, anyway" sent a far more powerful message than our weekly pep talks on quality.

Most of the time, people believe that managers reward those actions that they really value. When we recognize perfect attendance or praise people for accurate paperwork, people conclude that we must value attendance or paperwork. When we criticize those who complain about the quality of incoming supplies or outgoing products, people conclude that quality is not important to us. No matter how much we talk about quality and customer service, if we reward actions that detract from quality and customer service, our actions speak far louder than our words.

When you change your organization to make it more competitive, more flexible, more quality conscious, you *must* be sure that you reward the behavior that you really want. If you want the flexibility and rapid response time that groups will provide, you must be sure that you reward, not only flexibility and rapid responses, but also each person's contribution to the group effort, not his or her individual achievements. The behavior that you reward must be consistent with making the *groups* capable of reaching the overall organizational goals.

We will look more closely at the issue of group rewards later in the chapter. For now, some of the issues that we need to consider are the types of rewards that exist already within your organization, the complicated questions relating to monetary compensation, the unit of analysis for the distribution of rewards, and the type of formal pay system that might be appropriate for you.

Types of Rewards

Rewards fall into two basic categories: intrinsic, or those that derive from the actual performance of work; and extrinsic, or those that come from the organization, based on some standard such as performance, level of skill, or length of service.

Intrinsic Rewards.   If you have done a thorough analysis and followed the sociotechnical systems design principles, one characteristic of your new organization structure should be that it provides work that is intrinsically rewarding. Several management experts (Deci 1975; Herzberg 1966) have concluded that these built-in rewards are what actually motivate people to excel.

Volunteer organizations are experts at intrinsic motivation or intrinsic rewards. Often, volunteers who do difficult or tedious work could never be paid sufficiently for their efforts, but intrinsic rewards supply them with the motivation to continue. People generally do volunteer work because they get a kick out of it. Sometimes, they get direct feedback from the people whom they are working to help. Such is often the case when they work with those who benefit from their volunteer efforts. The response of the clients with whom they work makes volunteers feel good about their performance. Work with scout troops, in hospitals, or in youth organizations are examples of volunteer opportunities that provide intrinsic rewards in the form of feedback from clients.

Volunteer work can also be rewarding because volunteers can see that progress is being made as a direct result of their efforts. Crafts projects or building projects are examples here. The reward is simply the satisfaction of completion. Making a playground for the neighborhood, knitting a sweater for a friend, building a dollhouse for a child are rewarding in and of themselves. Seeing the finished product is the real reward, even before the recipient says thank you.

The work within the organization should be rewarding in this same manner. People should be able to see how their efforts contribute to the completion of a whole task or a coherent portion of a project. Sometimes, they will have face-to-face contact with customers, either internally or externally, who will provide them with direct feedback on their performance. Often, the work itself will provide them with such feedback. They will be able to see as soon as they have done something whether it is right or wrong. They can correct their own mistakes immediately, so that they have control over making sure that the final product or service is itself correct. Under these circumstances, the satisfaction of doing a good job provides intrinsic motivation to continue to perform well.

Because intrinsic motivation comes from the work itself, it is not something that you can add once you have finished designing your organization: It must be built from the start. Bowling again provides a good illustration. In a standard bowling team, all the members are motivated to do well. Watching the ball roll down the alley and knock over the pins provides the bowlers with immediate feedback on their performance. The motivation that individuals receive to do better all the time is also consistent with continual improvement of the league's standing. You want that same kind of congruency in your organizations. If people work better individually, their improvements should contribute to the team's effort, and the team's efforts should contribute to the organization's overall goals.

In the bowling example in Chapter 4, when a curtain is placed between the bowler and the pins, neither the ball rollers nor the pin setters receive much feedback, sense of accomplishment, or intrinsic motivation from the design of the game. In this situation, there is little that you can do to add on intrinsic motivation. As we discussed in Chapter 4, even paying people for doing their jobs better may not improve the overall performance of either the team or the league, because each person is responsible for only a small portion of the whole task.

Extrinsic rewards. Extrinsic rewards are generally associated with compensation or some tangible return for a person's efforts. They can also be the intangible rewards that come from a pat on the back or the congratulations that organization members exchange. These intangible rewards are valuable; they provide positive reinforcement for positive efforts. In many cases, they may come spontaneously from others in the organization. In other cases, people can be trained to give each other positive reinforcement.

The more tangible extrinsic rewards, such as compensation, are problematic under traditional structures and remain so even in more innovative, team-oriented structures. To grasp the connection between compensation and outcome in a team-oriented structure, it is first necessary to understand the nature of compensation.

Compensation

Compensation issues can be uncomplicated tremendously if you decide up front whether you are going to classify wages and salaries as a motivator or as a payment for services received. Let's look at each of these strategies separately.

Compensation as a Motivational Tool.   Trying to devise a compensation system that will motivate people can lead to frustration and disappointment. One of the advantages of a sociotechnical systems approach is that you need not rely on money to motivate. Your new structure should be designed so that the roles people play, the jobs they do, and the feedback they receive provide motivation. You then pay for the results.

Management experts like Herzberg (1966) and Deci (1975) have documented fairly persuasively that money will not motivate people to perform. Management practitioners, too, are very much aware of the limitations of money as a motivator. You can be fairly certain, for example, that, after months of enforced overtime, workers either believe in what they are doing or are motivated by some goal other than money, because, after a while, time and a half or even double time for overtime is not what brings them in every weekend and keeps them late during the week.

The weakness in many compensation systems is that they try to leverage the motivational power of the dollar. Since the dollar alone has little power to motivate beyond the bare minimum required, such systems often do not work as planned.

Compensation in Exchange for Value.   A more appropriate way to view compensation in a sociotechnical systems approach is as payment for services that have some value to the organization. Defining value as "getting what you pay for" is not particularly new. Normally, however, in terms of compensation, we approach this idea through the back door, so to speak. We establish a wage or salary that we are willing to pay, based on whatever criteria that we are using, and then we develop a management system to guarantee that we get our money's worth from that wage or salary.

In a sociotechnical systems approach, when the design of the work itself becomes the motivating factor, we need to look at getting what we pay for from another angle: We need to look at what value is being added by the labor involved. If the work being done has no value to the organization, it is worth nothing and its performance should probably be questioned. If too many jobs add little or no value to the outcome, you may need to examine further your organization's structure and job design.

Identifying the Value You Receive. An important aspect of designing a compensation system for a new organization structure is to identify clearly the value added by the people you are going to pay. In particular, if the value added by people in the new structure will be different from the value those same people added in the old, you need to identify that difference.

Consider a manufacturing firm that is organized rather traditionally, where individuals perform specific, differentiated tasks in a sequential pattern. These individuals are organized loosely into departments or sections, and the sections are also related sequentially to each other. When one section finishes its set of collective tasks, the product is passed on to another section, where individuals add to it or use it as a subassembly in their work. This process continues until a finished product emerges at the end of the entire sequence.

Now suppose this manufacturing organization, like many today, decides to change its structure so that tighter groups of individuals work together, mutually adjusting their performance to complete an entire product. Each group or team would be responsible for making its product or service the best that it could be. The stronger the competition among these teams to outperform each other, the better the overall organizational result. Individuals within the teams perform whatever tasks are necessary to be sure that the product is built to the customer's satisfaction.

Under the traditional structure, the value added by each individual is some incremental stage of a complete product. Sometimes, this

Figure 6–1. Factors to Consider in Calculating the Value Added by a Team.

• What is the value added to the product or service by the team?

What is the value of the product or service when it leaves the team?
What is the value of the inputs (other than labor performed by the team members)?

• What ancillary functions now are being performed by the team members that previously had required a separate function?

Production planning?
On-the-job training?
Quality control?
Budget monitoring?
Industrial engineering?
How would you calculate the value of these functions?
What would the loss be if the functions were not performed?

---

value has already been calculated by the experts in accounting, who use it to determine the value of work-in-process. In terms of pay, each increment is interpreted to be roughly equal to each other increment. In some cases, a task may take longer to learn or require more skill, and, traditionally, a worker performing such a task is considered to add more value than does an individual performing a less skilled job. Pay practices have reflected this differentiation.

Under the new team structure, the value added by each individual is less clear. The value added by the team, however, may be more clear. Figure 6–1 provides a checklist of some factors to consider when determining the value added by a team. If a team makes an entire product, the value added is the difference between the cost of the raw materials used and the value of the finished product. Some percentage of that value belongs to the stockholders in exchange for the capital that they have invested. A portion of the value may be needed for support functions that the team cannot provide itself. In many cases, however, the team will provide much of its own support. Detailed production planning, for instance, is often done by the teams, as will be quality assurance when they are in full swing. Even the training of new employees often is taken over by the team.

The issue now becomes how to determine exactly how much of the value added belongs to the members of the team and how to apportion that value among the members. Before we look at that more closely, further discussion of the team as the building block of the organization is in order. Most of us have had little experience with organizations built around teams, so we are less familiar with compensation systems geared toward team structure.

The Team as the Unit of Analysis

If you have moved from individuals to groups as the building blocks, an important piece of your supporting structure becomes making sure that rewards use groups as the level of analysis. Since pay and rewards ultimately accrue to individuals, the key is to be sure that individuals receive their rewards based on their contributions to the teams of which they are members. The notion of connections again becomes important. Individual performance must be connected to team performance, and team performance must be connected to the overall performance of the organization. To do otherwise will cause a discontinuity and channel efforts in opposite or random directions.

We have already seen that value added can be determined fairly easily if the teams are the unit that we analyze. Determining each team member's contribution, however, is less straightforward. At one extreme, each team can be given a lump sum that they divide according to their own determination of who has contributed what. At the other extreme, a system can be devised that uses standard criteria for determining individual contribution to group effort. Either of these arrangements represents a fairly dramatic change from the current system in most organizations.

While having each group determine how to distribute their rewards among the members may be the method you will ultimately want to use, it requires a fairly mature group whose members have already learned how to deal with the issues that they may encounter, such as how to handle an individual who is not performing, how to train its members to become good performers, how to solve problems as a group, and so forth. There are probably better points at which to begin.

Individual Accountability to Teams.   Your first imperative when designing a reward system in an organization built on teams is to see that each individual is accountable to a team and each team is accountable for its own results. The design standards discussed in Chapter 5 should have led you to this type of structure, and the reward systems must now support it. This is an absolute rule—not a guide: You cannot have effective teams if individuals within them are accountable directly to the organization or to any entity outside the team. The power of the team relies in great part on its being able to control its own results and on building commitment to those results among its membership. If team members are accountable to someone or some structure outside the team, the power of the group to get results is diminished.

Matrix organizations frequently suffer from this problem. People are assigned to functional managers who mete out their salary increases and review their performance, but they actually work with a project manager on a project team. This arrangement often divides loyalty. On the other hand, there is accountability to the functional manager who will reward performance and take care of promotions; on the other hand, there is some sense of responsibility to the project. If no conflicts ever occur between the two, the individual can function effectively. However, resources are often scarce in matrix organizations, and conflicts frequently result, putting the individual in a very awkward position. When directions from the functional manager and directions from the project manager clash, the outcome in terms of individual behavior is not always clearly predictable.

You want to avoid this two-master syndrome in the optimum organization. Each team should be working toward overall organizational goals; each individual should be accountable to a single team for his or her results. Teams should have clear areas of responsibility and be accountable for their own results. If you find too much overlap when you complete your structure, you may want to make some early revisions. If you followed the guideline that we set out earlier and designed your new organization so that relationships within groups were reciprocal or mutually interdependent and relationships between groups were pooled or fairly independent of each other, you should not have this problem and your reward systems will be much easier to design.

Team Accountability to the Organization.   Think about a traditional assembly organization in which each section produces a subassembly and passes it on to the next section in a series of sequential operations. Human nature being what it is, if each of these sections develops any team spirit or group cohesiveness, they will all tend to compete with each other for positive recognition, resources, or any other rewards that they perceive. This competition usually does not serve the overall goals of the organization very well; instead, it results in finger pointing, one-upsmanship, and bickering over turf issues.

In an organization designed according to a sociotechnical systems approach, groups ideally have reciprocal relationships within themselves but pooled relationships with other groups. When natural competition occurs between such teams, the result is a better product. The overall goals of the organization are thus well served by the competition. For this to happen, however, every team must be working toward organizational goals. To create other dependencies is to encourage empire building and working at cross-purposes.

These guidelines may seem self-evident, but organizations do get redesigned with less than optimum structures. Once again, remember the English coal mines discussed in Chapter 1. Before the technological improvements, each team did whatever was necessary to extract as much coal as possible from the mine. After the changes, only one group in three actually worked at and was rewarded for extracting coal; the others were rewarded for activities that did not always support the organization's goal as planned.

Another example that comes to mind is an organization that provided financial and management systems services to a variety of clients. In restructuring the organization, the manager moved from departments that were organized around the types of clients served to departments organized around the types of tasks that they performed. As a result, he created departments that were functional in nature and tended to operate sequentially, so that one department could perform a task for all the services and all the clients who subscribed to each service.

Under the old structure, when departments were organized more along client lines, each client knew exactly whom to call with questions or problems. Since that relationship would no longer exist under the new structure, the manager created a customer-service department to handle all questions, requests, and complaints from clients. Customer-service representatives who took calls and those that researched problems or passed along requests belonged to separate subdivisions of the department.

The organization encountered its first difficulty when, instead of responding directly to customer calls as they had in the past, internal departments found themselves responding to another internal department—customer service. A rule of thumb in most organizations is that internal groups rarely have as much clout as the customer. Thus, where entire departments previously had felt responsible for particular clients, they now found themselves responsible for a function or a task that seemed to have little connection to an end user. In addition, individuals were now accountable both to the department in which they worked and to the new customer-service department.

How were managers going to evaluate performance in the new organization? Would individuals be rewarded for performing the task that their department demanded of them or for responding to every customer-service request for information or help? How would the ability to serve the customer be reflected in the reward system?

This example illustrates how the structure itself can complicate the reward system. If you find yourself creating a Rube Goldberg reward system, you may want to reexamine your structure to see whether it is supporting adequately your organization's goals and mission.

The Best Pay System for Your Organization

Very simply, the best pay system for your organization will compensate individuals for their contributions to a particular team that produces positive results for the organization. To achieve such a system, you must be sure that you are paying for what you want to receive in return and that everyone understands what this is. If your pay system is based on attendance, for instance, you will find yourself managing attendance. On the other hand, if you make it clear that you are paying for results, and each person understands what he or she is expected to accomplish, you will find yourself worrying more about results than about absenteeism and tardiness. Admittedly, there are laws that govern the payment of overtime to certain classes of employees, but, even in those cases, concentrating on results will make it more apparent to your employees that you expect something in return for the wages and salaries that you pay them.

How you apportion wages and salaries is important only in that it should not interfere with the results that you want the organization to achieve. For example, if your current salary structure provides for fairly narrow job classifications and strict differentiation between levels of skill, it may limit your ability to build work groups that are flexible and able to respond quickly to changing customer needs or business demands.

A Look at Skill-Based Compensation.   Because the need for flexibility has increased in most businesses over the last ten years, some organizations have experimented with skill-based pay systems, which base individual pay on the number or variety of different skills that a person uses. In some of the systems, skills are considered to be relatively equal, and pay is differentiated only according to the number of skills that an individual has. In others, some skills are seen as being worth more, and individuals get proportionately more pay for possessing those along with their other skills.

Skill-based compensation systems have their drawbacks, just as any compensation system does. Some of the drawbacks cited are that people will gain skills to get the pay and then fail to use them on a regular basis; administration of these plans is often cumbersome and requires some method of testing for skill ability; and those people who top out by learning all the skills may have nothing else to motivate them to continue working.

Most of these drawbacks can be addressed. When people acquire skills and do not use them, the problem may be that the organization does not need quite that much flexibility. If this is the case, it should be recognized early in the program, and some limit should be placed on the number of skills for which you are willing to pay any given individual. If you identify clearly the value that you receive for the services rendered by employees, you are less likely to end up paying for more flexibility than you need.

Administration of the plan can be simplified by diversifying the responsibility for testing. If one person is expected to administer the plan and maintain testing capabilities for an entire organization, the task can become burdensome. However, individual groups can be taught to be responsible for the performance of their members. If administration continues to be too complicated, the details of the basic plan probably need some work.

When compensation is used as motivation, the problem of topping out is serious; when motivation comes from the work itself, however, this problem is less pressing. In an organization that allows teams to share in the gains to which they have contributed, for example, topping out is less apt to become an issue, since teams can become better and better at what they do and earn more in the process.

Conclusions About Rewards

In good organizational structure, jobs and opportunities carry intrinsic motivation. Extrinsic motivation is most powerful in the form of positive reinforcement from others in the organization. Compensation issues are simplified if compensation is seen as an exchange for value received rather than as an instrument to motivate employees. When it is seen as an exchange for value, compensation becomes a question of identifying the value that you want and paying for it.

POLICIES AND PROCEDURES

While compensation may be viewed as a policy or a procedure, there are other policies and procedures in most organizations that need to be reevaluated from time to time. A restructuring effort is an ideal occasion to reexamine your organization's policies and procedures and shake out those that are interfering with the ability to achieve results. For example, if the purpose of your new structure is to make your organization more flexible, policies that allow no room to maneuver or procedures that allow no deviation will tend to interfere with the results that you want.

This section focuses on how you can determine the value of an existing policy or procedure so that you can decide whether to leave it, change it, or eliminate it. Budgets and promotions will be examined in greater detail, because these policies often need to be changed following a restructuring project.

Determining the Value of a Policy or Procedure

The rule that applies to compensation applies to other organizational policies as well. That is, you should examine the value of each procedure or policy and determine two things: (1) what is the policy or procedure causing people to do, and (2) is that what you want them to do? Figure 6–2 provides a series of questions that you may find helpful in examining your current policies and procedures.

Many years ago, I was in an organization that paid a great deal of attention to attendance. Absences were counted each month, and those who had "too many" were counseled about their records. The policy

Figure 6–2.   Determining the Value of a Policy or Procedure.

• What problem was the policy or procedure originally meant to fix?

Does that problem still exist?
Will the problem return if the policy is eliminated or changed?

• Have any subsequent policies mitigated the effects or clarified the intent of this policy?

If so, what are they?

• What is this policy or body of policies supposed to cause people to do?

What are people actually doing?
Is this something that you want them to do?
Under what conditions would people do what you intend without a policy to guide them?
Are any of those conditions present in the new organization?

---

of trying to regulate attendance was, in retrospect, questionable, since no customers were flocking to our doors because we had people with perfect attendance. However, that aspect aside, another quirk in the policy created some interesting behavior.

That quirk had to do with the length of absences. Anything longer than three days became a disability. For some strange reason, disabilities did not count against your attendance record. You will have guessed already that this policy encouraged people with attendance problems to extend their absences to four days, thereby converting them to disabilities and wiping them off their records.

Did this policy have any value? From the customer's point of view, probably not. All the customer wanted was a reasonably priced product that worked. Who made it or how long it took to produce was irrelevant except as it related to the actual results. What did the policy cause people to do? It caused those who already had poor attendance records to stay out longer each time they were absent. Is that what we wanted them to do? Definitely not.

The chances are that if a policy or procedure causes people to play games to get around it, it will not be any more supportive of the new structure than it was of the old.

Budgets

In a team-oriented structure, teams must be responsible for their own budgets. In addition, positive effects in one budget should not produce negative effects in another budget. While these guidelines seem simple, they frequently are overlooked.

Give Teams Budget Responsibility   Making each team responsible for its own budget is really making each team responsible for conserving its own resources. Budgets do not grow out of proportion when they become the responsibility of those who use them. On the contrary, they are frequently used with greater discretion when those who need the resources are also responsible for using them wisely.

In one organization that was changing its structure from a traditional hierarchy to a flatter arrangement with semiautonomous work groups, one of the first responsibilities that was given to the teams was that of allocating and controlling their own overtime. This happened to be an older organization, with a work force in its mid-fifties, where overtime was still coveted. Yet, when the teams were confronted with the reality of the cost of overtime, the amount that they allowed their members to work dropped immediately. In a very short time, they began accomplishing all their work—and eventually more—in straight time with little or no need for overtime. In the past, overtime was something the company paid for; now, overtime was something that came out of the teams' budgets. The same budgets were identical to those under which their supervisors had operated, but, for the first time, the people who needed to get the job done also had responsibility over their budgets. They quickly found other ways to get their work done during normal working hours.

As managers, we may find the budget problem easier to understand when we consider health care rather than our own organizations; the same principles apply. When consumers began complaining about the high cost of hospitalization, many hospitals discovered that doctors had no idea what procedures cost. They simply ordered the procedures that they would like to have done. Even the hospitals had not attempted to hold down costs, because insurance companies were paying the bills. In organizations, as long as those who are spending money stay within limits, no one usually bothers them about how much they are spending. If the supervisor or manager is considered responsible for the budget, the group responsible for doing the work often has no sense of fiscal responsibility. Sometimes, even those spending the money are not aware of the costs involved. But when teams become responsible for their own budgets, they can see the limits and control their own costs. In many cases, the benefits to the organization begin to accrue immediately.

Avoid Interdependencies.   The cardinal rule in setting up budgets, as it is in designing organizations, is to avoid interdependencies. Budget interdependencies exist when, each time a given team has to accomplish a task, several courses of action are open to them to get a result, one of which would result in a negative effect, or an expenditure, to their budget, while another would result in a negative effect, or an expenditure, to someone else's budget. This frequently is the case in sequential operations. If something goes wrong in a subassembly, the temptation often is to pass the problem along to the next group. This is especially true in win-lose situations, when there is no reward for fixing a problem, but some cost is involved.

It often is possible to turn these in to win-win situations, but tremendous communication and coordination between teams or groups is usually required to work out solutions that are mutually beneficial. That level of intergroup coordination generally has little value to the organization and rarely is necessary, since an appropriate structure and appropriate budget arrangement can solve the problem far more easily.

If teams are accountable for their own expenditures, their own budgets, and their bottom lines continually are affected by situations outside their control, they will become frustrated with the effort of acting responsibly. Furthermore, if teams can affect each other's bottom lines they will spend as much—or more—time trying to play games with the budget as they do working to get positive results for the organization.

Promotions.

Another policy issue that you should examine is the promotion policy. You must be sure that the people whom you promoted under the old structure and the reasons for which you promoted them are still supportive of the results that you hope to achieve with the new structure.

If your old structure was built around individuals, chances are that you promoted those individuals who were outstanding in their own right. In an organization built around teams, however, the primary criteria for promotion, as for rewards, should be contribution to the efforts of the team. Sometimes, these people are the same in either structure. On occasion, though, the high flyer is not a team player, but someone who may actually detract from overall team performance. If the organization is aligned properly, detracting from team performance also detracts from overall organization performance. By the same token, contributing to team performance contributes to overall organization performance. The people you want to reward and promote are those who contribute the most to overall organization performance through their teams.

If you have a written policy on promotion, this change will be relatively simple to make. However, my experience is that many organizations have no clear-cut policy. In these cases, the change will be largely cultural. People will need to learn what the new values are and that they will be promoted for adhering to those values. Likewise, those who make promotion decisions will need to understand the new organization values. This may be an area that you will have to monitor closely in the early days of your new structure. You may find that paying extra attention to promoting people whose behavior is congruent with the overall organization's objectives is well worth the effort.

TRAINING

Almost any change that you make in an organization must be accompanied by some training to bring people up to speed in the behaviors and skills that will be required of them. Restructuring—a major change, indeed—is no exception. Three basic areas require training:

1. People must understand the organization goals and how the new organization carries out those goals.
2. People must understand their own roles in the new organization.
3. People must learn some new skills, both to work with groups and to perform the new tasks necessary to achieve the required results.

Organizational Goals

When you are counting on individuals to work together toward certain results, they must understand those results so that they can make decisions about appropriate priorities. If they have budget responsibility, they must understand what is important and what is not important in terms of allocating the budget. They must understand what the customer wants and how their organization has chosen to fill the customer's needs.

Understanding the organization's goals becomes especially critical if you have eliminated layers of management in your restructuring effort. Suddenly, the people who had the maps are gone, and those who now must reach the goals and achieve the results need to know what the destination is and how to get there.

As important as an understanding of overall direction is, even more important is an understanding of what those goals mean to each individual and group within the organization. Laying out the broad purpose or mission of each group can be a valuable lesson for you as a manager. If, for example, you discover a group whose purpose is not particularly related to the overall organization goal, you may want to question the new structure. Where did that group come from? What value does it return to the organization? Can the functions it performs be accomplished within a more results-oriented group?

Role Clarification

Closely related to the issue of goals is that of understanding the roles that individuals and teams play in carrying out the organization's mission. Some of these roles may have changed dramatically under the new structure.

The Role of Managers.   Particularly if you have moved to a team-oriented structure, the role of the managers in your new organization will be different from their roles in a more traditional hierarchical structure. The classic functions of managers—directing, controlling, planning, organizing—are no longer appropriate in a flatter organization; many of these activities are assumed by the teams as they become responsible for their own results. Teams direct their members and control their resources. Teams do the detailed planning of the work and organize the processes and resources.

Managers will now tend to play an integrative role. Where teams must interact or coordinate their efforts with each other, managers will serve as coordinators or integrators, facilitators more than directors. Their new role is to make the system work so that it does not interfere with achieving the results.

The Role of Team Members.   Individuals who operated independently in the old structure will find themselves working more closely with each other in a team-oriented structure. In many cases, they will take on the functions of directing, controlling, planning, and organizing that have been abandoned by the managers. They must understand how their roles fit into the overall scheme of things within the new structure. And, as we have said, they must understand what you expect of them.

New Skills

New roles involve new skills for both managers and team members. Both groups must learn new task skills and new process skills in order to do their work. While no attempt will be made here to outline complete training programs for these areas, both process skills and task skills deserve a few words.

Process Skills.   Process skills involve the knowledge and ability to carry out work within the new team-based structure. This category includes problem solving in groups, facilitation skills, and interpersonal skills.

   Problem Solving.   When people are grouped together in teams, they are interdependent and must adjust their activities mutually in order to reach goals and achieve results. They must be able to solve problems quickly as they occur, and they must be able to do this in a variety of formal and informal groups. Each individual cannot go off in a separate direction and come up with a solution; all must know how to work together to solve problems. This problem-solving ability provides much of the flexibility and quick response that you need to be competitive in today's environment.

   Many techniques exist for problem solving in groups, and most of them are fairly simple to learn. A number were even compiled into books when quality circles began flourishing in this country. The training can be quite effective when it is applied to functioning work groups and they are allowed to try the process on their own problems.

Facilitation Skills. Managers, particularly, will need to be able to facilitate the work of groups. Facilitating a group is exactly what it sounds like: It involves helping a group to solve problems and get things accomplished. During times when groups must work closely with each other, during group problem solving, for instance, a facilitator in the form of a manager or leader can often unstick the group and keep it moving toward its goal.

Facilitation calls for more listening and questioning than is usual in more traditional management functions. Much of this training is readily available and has been outlined in books on the subject. Quality-circle literature also generally includes some information on group facilitation.

Interpersonal Skills. People who work closely with other people need the skills to do so. Some people seem to be born with the skills that allow them to get along with others quite naturally. Other people need some reminding. Those who were traditional managers prior to the change may need some special coaching in listening and communicating skills. Individual team members who used to work in fairly isolated surroundings may also need some help in learning how to communicate clearly and listen to what others have to say.

Among the interpersonal skills that you may want to provide is some training in how to give positive reinforcement. As behavior changes in desired ways, both peers and bosses need to reward that behavior so that it will be repeated. Sometimes, a simple thank you or a smile is enough, but some people will need reminding even in this area. Positive reinforcement is seen as unnecessary by those who think that just doing the job is no reason for special attention. This is an assumption that you may want to work to change.

Task Skills. If part of the organizational goal is to become more flexible, both managers and team members will have to learn new tasks in order to be as flexible as possible. As a prelude to learning new skills, team members may need to learn how to teach skills to others. As people expand their knowledge base, someone must teach them new skills. Those who already have the skills are the best source of information.

To make that transfer from one person to another, however, you must be sure that some people have the skills necessary to teach others how to do a job. If you have a training department, its best use will probably be to provide these skills to some team members, who can then pass the knowledge on. In this way, the new system becomes self-supporting. This type of training is often referred to as "training the trainer" or "job-instruction training."

SELECTION

Who selects people and what criteria are used are two areas that may need attention in your restructured organization. While this book does not pretend to offer a complete guide to selection and hiring, a brief discussion of each of these practices is in order.

Who Makes the Initial Selection?

In a number of organizations that are built around teams, the personnel department performs only an initial screening of job applicants. Final selection for employment is left up to the teams themselves. There are both benefits and drawbacks to this approach.

One benefit is that the teams retain more control over the input to their processes. Teams' ability to control their input is an important feature of a sociotechnical systems design. If the principle applies to the selection of their own members, they will probably work more diligently to bring newcomers up to speed and make them an integral part of the team. Group cohesion in a high-performance team can be valuable to the organization.

A drawback, however, is that cliques can develop if teams are allowed to choose every new member. Particularly in untrained teams, this can lead to the selection of people based on idiosyncratic criteria. Teams can develop an internal homogeneity that may hamper their creativity and limit their collective point of view.

I saw an example of this problem a number of years ago, when I was the human-resource manager in an organization that was closing down. Because we had been the major industrial employer and had paid the highest wages in the area, we had a reputation for having only the best employees. The only other industrial employer in town was a new plant that processed chemicals for the health-food industry. It was organized around semiautonomous work groups. While the personnel department did the initial screening of applicants, the teams made the final selection. It soon became apparent that, although our handicapped and minority employees were passing the personnel department's screen and being put into their hiring pool, few of them were being selected by the teams, which tended to choose attractive, youngish white women and nice-looking, youngish white men. Eventually, the company had to educate its teams in the finer points of selection and legal requirements.

Criteria for Selection

You may want to modify your selection process to include some skills or abilities that you have not sought before. For example, you will want people who can work with others. Among the interpersonal aptitudes that you might seek is the ability to listen and to communicate. You also will want people who have the ability to learn new skills, so you may want to add flexibility and problem solving to the criteria that you use in your initial selection procedures. While most of these skills can be taught to some extent and you may certainly have to teach them to your existing work force, you may decide that you could save some training time if you select new employees who already have some of these skills and abilities.

One of the most important things to remember is that a change in the rules of your organization may change the skills and abilities that you need. Your challenge will be to apply the new criteria equally to all applicants and to be sure that your criteria do not eliminate unfairly any particular group or class of people. One way to develop the new criteria may be to involve your steering group or a special task force of team members who have acquired some experience with the new structure.

In retrofit situations, unless your business is expanding rapidly or your attrition rate is extremely high, it is unlikely that you will need to add large numbers of people. Your new organization should be more efficient and more effective; you will probably find that you can do more work with fewer people. In other words, if you are redesigning an existing organization, you may not need to face the issue of selection procedures and criteria for quite a while. You should give more initial attention to training your current work force and measuring the results that your newly restructured organization is achieving.

SUMMARY

Optimizing your organization requires that you support the new structure through your reward systems, policies and procedures, skills training, and selection procedures. If any part of your new structure is not supporting optimum results, its value must be questioned, and you may have to make additional changes to keep your organization moving in the right direction.

7 MEASURING THE RESULTS

What we must decide is perhaps how we are valuable, rather than how valuable we are.

> Edgar Z. Friedenberg, "The Impact of the School," *The Vanishing Adolescent*, 1959

As managers, very few of us would undertake a major project without setting some goals and being able to determine afterward whether we had been successful or not. Organizational changes also need some criteria for determining success. Frequently, the measurement systems already in place are not sufficient both to gauge success and to provide the feedback that the organization needs to improve continually. As a result, measurement is another issue that must be addressed in an organization restructuring. In this chapter, we will examine some of the reasons why measurement is important and what areas should be measured.

WHY MEASURE?

Basically, you measure results to find out how well you are doing. Perhaps the better question is, "Why do you need to know how you are doing?" One of the reasons might be that you need to provide additional justification for the change you have just instituted, if not to others, then for your own peace of mind. You also need to know your status so that you can continue to improve. A third reason is that feedback is an integral part of the open systems model, and, in

147

many cases, you need good measurements in order to provide feedback on results. Each of these reasons deserves further discussion.

Justification

While change for the sake of change may appeal to many people, most of us must justify the changes that we make, both to ourselves and to our shareholders or our bosses. When either one of these latter groups asks you how things are in your new organization, you cannot answer simply that they seem to be going well; you must be able to demonstrate how well they are going. To do that you need to be able to measure results.

For justification purposes, the measures that you used before the change may be quite appropriate. Sales or services billed, income after tax, operating profit, and the like may be fine for providing feedback to upper management or shareholders. These measurements are familiar to managers and shareholders; they will be better able to compare results if you use the same yardstick after the change as you did before it. In fact, when you are measuring to gain support for the changes you have made, you should be sure that you have comparable pre-change measures.

Continuous Improvement

Measuring to monitor continuous improvement is very important. The business environment in the years ahead promises to be no less turbulent than it has been in the recent past. Under constantly changing conditions, few organizations can afford to remain static, resting on the status quo. Most will need to demonstrate continuous improvement in all areas.

You cannot improve continually if you do not know where you have been and where you are currently. In addition, you need to be able to tell when and where adjustments to your new organization structure are necessary. Measurements are necessary to determine when results are less than optimum, as well as to show when they are right on target.

In most cases, the broad measurements that you have been tracking on a regular basis will suffice to determine overall performance. But post-change measures with no comparable pre-change information are also adequate to show continuing improvement, although you will have no data to illustrate the initial improvement brought about by the changes. You may want to choose some new measurements that are similar to those used by your competitors. If your competitors measure market share, for instance, perhaps you should do the same. You also definitely should measure those aspects of your business that are critical to your new mission or strategy. For example, if your goal is to be the low-cost producer in your industry, you must focus your measurement efforts on your costs. If your goal is to provide the highest quality product or services, your measurement must focus on quality and customer satisfaction.

Feedback as Part of an Open System

One of the essential elements of an organization structured as an open system is the feedback loop. In a well-designed organization, the work itself provides some feedback, which enhances intrinsic motivation, as we discussed in Chapter 6. In the process of performing their work, people discover either that something is correct and they can continue or that something is wrong and they must correct it before they proceed. In either case, they have a sense of control and accomplishment.

In addition to this built-in feedback, other feedback or measurements must be devised to let people know where they stand. Teams cannot be expected to monitor their own operations if they cannot measure them. Measurements and feedback become critical to achieving optimum results.

When teams or individuals have no feedback on their performance, they generally tend to overestimate how well they are doing. If you have ever heard or seen an audio or video recording of yourself making a speech, you understand how critical feedback is to improvement. Until you see and hear yourself jingling change in your pockets or filling all your pauses with awkward "ah's," you usually do not even realize where you need to improve. So it is in organizations. Teams and individuals need feedback. They need to know how they are doing in relation to their own past performance and in relation to the performance of others.

Many of the measurements that organizations track traditionally have less meaning at the level of the team or individual than they do for monitoring overall organizational performance or informing the shareholders of current status. For example, you can give teams hour-by-hour updates on the current sales billed, income after taxes, or stock price, but, normally, that data tells them little about their own performance and what they can do to improve. Special attention must be paid to developing usable measures for teams and individuals so that they can monitor their own results.

WHAT TO MEASURE

A general rule of thumb in deciding what aspects of your organization to measure is that you should measure only that which is important. While this rule may seem self-evident, in practice, organizations do not always adhere to it. Measuring attendance, which we have mentioned before, is a good example. Attendance tells you only whether people are at work, not how well they are performing or what results they are achieving.

Focusing on Results

As we have said earlier, in an organization based on sequential relationships, such as an assembly operation, attendance is important, because plans are made based on all the stations being staffed. Even then, however, attendance is only an interim measure. What really counts is what comes off the end of the assembly line.

When an organization moves to teams and the internal relationships are reciprocal, measures must focus on results. Attendance becomes a team issue, not an organizationwide issue. If the team deems attendance to be important to results, it will track attendance; the chances are, however, that peer pressure to carry a fair share of the team's load virtually will eliminate the need for the team to track such interim measures. As for the organization, attendance simply is not its problem any more. All the organization needs to track are the results that the teams are achieving. In fact, it is critical for the organization to focus on results rather than on side issues.

The importance of measuring the right things was one of the lessons learned in the English coal mines, if you recall. There, they measured the number of holes drilled and the cubic area of undercutting, as well as the total tonnage extracted. The revealing measurement proved to be that of total tonnage extracted, which dropped. Had the tonnage increased, there would have been little reason for the owners to be concerned with a decrease in the number of holes drilled or the cubic area undercut.

We have already mentioned that, when something is measured, most people conclude that management values that activity. Generally, activities that are measured get done. If you focus on ancillary issues or interim measures instead of on results, people may apply themselves to unproductive or irrelevant tasks that contribute little to final results.

In today's challenging environment, most of us do not have time to worry about ancillary issues. We have our hands full achieving results and remaining competitive, and these are the areas where measurement should focus.

Devising Usable Measures

For the most part, measures should be usable at the point where people have some control over their outcome. Let me illustrate the need for useable measures with an anecdote. Several years ago, I was serving as a consultant to a manufacturing organization that was using a sociotechnical systems approach to restructure its operating units. One of the problems that it had identified in the analysis stage was that too many customers had complaints about quality. One of the goals for the new structure was to improve quality so that the organization would receive no more customer complaints. One of the tactics for improving quality was to create semiautonomous work groups and make them responsible for the quality of the products they made.

Overall, the company's products were relatively nontechnical and, as such, had no warranty provision. This meant that the organization had no warranty accrual and no convenient way of measuring how much it spent on defective products. The response to customer complaints in the past had been to send several employees to check out the problem and make things right with the customer. Sometimes, orders were remade, and new goods shipped. Both the labor and travel costs for the customer visits, as well as the material and labor costs for manufacturing a new product, were absorbed into the operations budget. Like most organizations, the company had no desire to highlight these costs for upper management or shareholder scrutiny.

After the first few months under the new structure, we all were confident that quality had improved. Each team was working to make sure that none of its product left the factory in any way flawed. There was a growing feeling of pride in accomplishment. Several customers, in fact, had sent letters and telegrams commenting on the excellent quality that they were seeing.

However, when the next financial statement was released, the controller burst our bubble by announcing that scrap costs were higher than they had ever been. The conclusion of the financial experts was that our quality had declined. We were puzzled, wondering why our quality seemed to be so much better but our quality costs were so much higher. It defied logic, until we realized that we had been measuring the wrong things. Scrap costs were indeed higher, because people were rejecting defective material, instead of using it and making do as they had done before. But the costs of field repair and replacement had always been absorbed in the operating budget, so there was no way to show improvement in that area. We were trapped temporarily by an obsolete set of financial measures that did not tell the whole story.

Measuring Meaningful Results.   This story points out the need for accounting experts to understand the new structure and how it works early in the process, because they will need to devise reports and measures to monitor results that reflect the goals that the organization wants to achieve. In many cases, results must be measured at intermediate stages, not just at the tail end of the process. You must be able to measure the results of each of the transformation processes in your newly restructured organization. These measurements must be meaningful, accounting for activities or output that contribute directly to results. They should monitor activities that the customers or the shareholders care about. The teams or individuals must also be able to use these measures to improve their results.

Often, teams will invent their own measures. They will track those items and activities that they have learned are important to achieving results. They should be encouraged to do this and given support to ensure that they create usable measures. You may need to pay special attention here to the very different roles played by the financial wizards and the people doing the actual work and to the kinds of things that teams choose to measure.

The questions in Figure 7–1 may serve as a convenient checklist

Figure 7–1. Criteria for Usable Measurements.

Does this measure provide usable feedback to the people who are directly responsible for improving the performance it reflects?

Does this measure reflect an activity that contributes directly to overall organizational results?

Would an improvement in this measure lead to an improvement in overall organizational results?

Would a decline in this measure lead to a decline in overall results?

Is the cost of providing this measure less than the value received from the feedback that it provides?

Is this measure something that your competitors use?

Is this measure something that your customers and/or your stockholders care about?

---

when you are evaluating a measure for its usefulness. If a measure is good, the answers to most of the questions will be affirmative.

Role of the Accountants. In most organizations, the financial department or accounting group originally is created to provide a support function. However, in many cultures, accountants begin to play a much more central role. Both Lee Iacocca (1984) and David Halberstam (1986) report that, at one point, the financial group at Ford was making major decisions about operations, much to the detriment of the overall organization. Sound marketing and production decisions took a backseat to strictly financial decisions, some of which had more to do with allocating resources to the preparation of reports than to the manufacture of cars. When operating units must defer to the financial people, something is turned upside down. But this predicament is not entirely uncommon.

As a manager, you may find that part of your job is to reverse the thinking that allows this situation to occur. You must move the financial group back into its support role. One of the first challenges that it must face is how to provide useful data to each of the operating units, whether those units are teams or individuals. The data received by the operating people must provide useful feedback that will help them to achieve the results that you need and to strive continually to improve those results. This may mean that your financial group will have to use more creativity to figure out how to measure some of the activities that teams will need to monitor.

One of the reasons that some items or activities are measured in organizations is that the data for those measures are readily available. With the proliferation of computers, anything that can be counted easily can be measured, and frequently is. But some of the more important data that we need to monitor may not be as easy to collect. Keep in mind that, if an activity can be done, it can be measured. Another point to remember is that results that are congruent with overall organization goals are probably important enough to be measured.

Role of the End Users.   One approach that may contribute to devising useful measures is to allow the people who need the information to help figure out how the data should be collected. They may know of data that are being collected and used in one way that could be revised to be more useful in another measure. They may also be able to supply information that currently is not being collected at all.

Aside from developing more useful measures, a secondary advantage accrues from involving the teams or individuals in identifying useful information and collecting data. The more closely people are involved in gathering data, the less suspicious they will be of its accuracy. When teams collect their own data to monitor their progress, the feedback that they receive is irrefutable. They cannot blame a bean counter for getting the wrong figures. They own the data that they collected, and they cannot deny what it tells them.

Team Measurements.   Especially when teams are newly formed, they will be interested, not only in their results, but in how they are developing as a team. While building high-performance teams is to the organization's advantage, measurements regarding the team process should be approached with caution.

In addition to producing results, the teams will improve in many of the processes that they use. They should, for example, become more adept at group problem solving. They should be able to accomplish more and more in shorter and shorter meetings. They should be able to make better decisions as they become more experienced. They should make continually better use of their human resources as people become more skilled in new tasks.

Improvement in any of these areas should result in improved out-come: higher productivity, better quality, lower costs. However, mon-itoring interim measurements, such as time spent in team meetings or length of time to solve a problem as a group, tends to put the emphasis in the wrong place. The purpose of the team is to achieve results, not to hold meetings in record time or reduce the problem-solving process to an automatic response. In fact, measuring these enabling activities may detract from results, and results are what the marketplace looks at, not the quality of a meeting or the number of people who got involved in solving a problem. If you hold teams responsible for the resources that they use, as we discussed in Chapter 6, and for the results that they achieve, they must improve their problem solving and task skills and monitor their attendance, not as ends in themselves, but as the means to achieve overall improvement in results.

Managers in the new organization will help teams and individuals examine their results and determine how they were achieved. If results are less than expected, for example, it becomes appropriate to look at the processes that the teams are using to obtain their results and to ask questions about how they are going about identifying and solving problems, how much time they are spending in meetings discussing problems, and how effective that time is. These interim measures are the whys of the results. After studying them, you can help the teams examine their own skills and how flexible or inflexible they have become so that they can see why final results are not as they should be.

SUMMARY

Most organizations discover that what gets measured, gets done. For that reason, any measurement in the optimum organization should focus on results. Where ancillary activities contribute to results, they should be examined only as a means to an end. When too much emphasis is placed on monitoring ancillary activities, they suddenly take on new importance and often become ends in themselves.

Usable measures may need to be developed jointly by the accounting experts and the task experts. When used as feedback, only those measures over which people have control are useful and meaningful; overall organizational measures, such as income after taxes or sales billed, are not ordinarily very useful to the teams and individuals who are charged with obtaining results. Moreover, the measures that are the easiest to make, such as attendance or time spent in meetings, may not contribute the most to the achievement of overall organization results.

8 CONTINUING THE IMPROVEMENT

Perpetual in-place fixing is the new order of things.
—Ian I. Mitroff, *Business Not as Usual*, 1987

Eliyahu Goldratt and Jeff Cox (1986), in their very unusual novel about a manufacturing plant, argue that it is impossible for the goal of a successful enterprise to be some fixed point that, when reached, will guarantee security. In today's competitive environment, the only viable goal is continuous improvement. Optimizing your organization is not a one-time project; it is an iterative process that you must work on continually, monitoring results and making changes and adjustments so that the system continues to function in balance with its own internal elements and with the environment.

The concept of ongoing change is sometimes difficult to accept, particularly if you like to have all the details nailed down as quickly as possible. But your marketplace and your business environment in general probably will not be static over the next decade or more: Most of us will have to do without permanency, at least at work, if our businesses are to survive into the twenty-first century.

In the last chapter, we talked about some of the aspects of your organization that must change to support your new structure, such as reward systems, skill levels for all employees, the roles of both managers and nonmanagers, and measurement systems. All of these may require continuous changes as the structure is modified over time to improve overall organizational performance; however, reward systems, team structures (if your design includes teams), and team memberships

157

deserve special attention in terms of ongoing change. Your own role as manager in the ongoing improvement of your organization also will require constant adaptation. In this final chapter, we will examine these subjects in greater detail.

REWARD SYSTEMS

At one time, the need to change and revise compensation systems was felt to indicate failure. Many of us thought that we ought to be able to find the perfect way to pay people under these innovative work structures. However, as time goes on, I am inclined to think that a perfect pay system for any work structure—innovative or traditional —is an impossible dream. In fact, we often hurt ourselves by living with the same system for years and years rather than admitting that we need to make changes.

In the late seventies, I found myself in a traditional smokestack industry trying to recruit computer systems analysts from the area around Boston's Route 128 Technology Belt. The work that we were doing could not compete with the new high-tech giants in terms of innovation and intrigue, but, even more damningly, our salary structure treated systems analysts slightly less well than mechanical engineers.

Our compensation system was clearly out of sync with the business realities of the labor supply, yet any attempts to change it were constantly overruled by those who had the power for approval—indeed, it was not even allowed to become an issue. The rules that we lived by dictated that we accept the existing pay structure. We operated under the assumption that this was a temporary condition that would work itself out.

Herein lies the biggest difference between pay systems in some of the newer, flatter, more flexible organizations and those in older, more hierarchical, more traditional organizations. In the more innovative organization structures, inefficiencies and inadequacies in the pay and reward systems are allowed to surface as legitimate issues so that changes can be made. The assumption under which they operate is that the internal processes, policies, and procedures must be adjusted constantly for the organization to maintain a competitive balance with its environment. As a result, organizations that have undergone structural changes and have already altered their compensation systems to support their new structures often find themselves reexamining the systems several years later and finding that they no longer serve their purpose. As external conditions change, internal conditions must change as well.

Skill-Based Pay Issues

One example of a compensation issue that arises from time to time in innovative organizations is the life cycle of a skill-based compensation system. When organizations install a skill-based compensation system to support the flexibility needed in their new structure, they often discover that, after several years, a certain percentage of the work force has learned the maximum number of skills and thus is receiving the highest pay level possible. This topping out is considered to render the entire system obsolete. Some people have even suggested that perhaps additional layers or skill levels should be added so that people can continue to earn more money.

Two things, however, often go unrecognized. First, people also top out under traditional pay systems; it is just less obvious. And second, pay falls into the general category of extrinsic rewards, as we discussed in Chapter 6, and, hence, is not a very powerful motivating factor to begin with.

The biggest problem here may not be that people cannot earn more money but that there is no room for further advancement. In fact, the ability to move higher probably has more motivating potential than the additional money in the paycheck. Other positions or other potential opportunities for growth and promotion often can substitute for an additional level of pay beyond those attained by learning as many skills as possible.

Another assumption that may get in our way when we consider pay and rewards is that we tend to think that the top of the salary or wage range is a goal that people set out to reach. While that may be true, if we create an organizational culture in which the goal is not some fixed target but continuous improvement, there is no such thing as topping out. There will always be room for improvement. If improvement is connected to a gainsharing plan, the compensation system can remain viable for longer. Linking improvements to pay also focuses efforts on the ultimate goal of continuous improvement.

Conclusions about Rewards

The two main points to remember about reward systems are that the work itself must continue to offer an intrinsic challenge to those who perform it and that the pay system with which you began is not sacred. As long as people understand why you are making changes and feel that the changes are appropriate and fair to all concerned, you can continue to improve the fit between the organization's mission, its structure, and its reward systems, which, in turn, will contribute to your goal of continuous overall improvement.

CHANGES IN THE TEAMS

Environmental and internal changes may cause you to reexamine the structure itself. When teams are involved, two aspects may need to be monitored: team structure and team membership.

Team Structure

Changes in your business environment, technology, or human-resource needs precipitated your first restructuring; there is no reason to believe that conditions in the future will not necessitate additional changes. If you have built your organization around teams, there will be a particular need to monitor the structure for continuing suitability. Flexibility and competitiveness are the watchwords here. If products or services change or if the technology used to produce and deliver your products or services change, you probably will not want to continue with precisely the same team structure with which you began. The same criteria that you used initially to design your new organization should be used continually to monitor its performance and maintain an appropriate structure.

Organizations built around teams often discover that certain tasks, products, or services may not require a team structure. Providing renewal parts is one example. As we mentioned in Chapter 4, this work often involves pooled relationships: Parts are stocked in some quantity and ordered by common stock numbers, regardless of the customer; individuals working independently, with well-designed work, good information, and appropriate feedback, can perform the task and accomplish the objectives without the complexity of a team. Yet, when some organizations discover this kind of situation in areas of their operations, they nevertheless adapt it to a team structure, as though they are reluctant to mix building blocks.

While maintaining teams where they are not appropriate may not cause problems, it certainly requires more effort than is necessary. If a loose federation of individuals can accomplish a task as well as a tightly knit team can, taking advantage of this option does not necessarily signal an inconsistency.

Consistency derives from using the same principles in designing the entire organization and communicating a clear vision to all organization members. If you have laid the groundwork well and involved as many people as possible in the design of your organization, adjustments and changes of this sort should come about fairly naturally. Those involved will understand—and may even suggest—the need for such changes.

Team Membership

If increased flexibility is one of your goals, you want to avoid any situation that encourages your new organization to be rigid in the face of changing business conditions. Members of high-performance teams can become so accustomed to working together that they begin to think alike and to see the world from similar perspectives. This homogeneity can eventually make them reluctant to accept changes in the way that they operate. They may become complacent, which can lead them to abandon their quest for improvement, or they may remain a high-performance team but no longer be doing what you want them to do. Rowing well in the wrong direction is worse than not rowing at all.

Most sociotechnical systems experts agree that there must be some degree of flexibility in the membership of teams. This can be encouraged through rotation of individuals from one team to another. Some organizations place so much emphasis on rotation that teams are structured to be of similar sizes and to involve the same length of time for learning skills, so that rotation between teams can be formal and planned. At specified intervals, a certain percentage of the organization's population rotates to different teams.

I am not convinced that rotation needs to be so formal nor that ideal structure should be sacrificed to gain more flexibility or mobility between teams. However, I do believe that people should be allowed and encouraged to move to other teams on a relatively regular basis. This belief is rooted in several concerns.

First of all, on occasion, there exist within organizations conflicts that euphemistically are referred to as personality clashes, although, fortunately, they are usually rare. They fall into two broad categories. In the first, clashes tend to follow the same people from one spot to another in the organization. When this is the case, the problem may lie with the individual and cannot be solved by a move to another team. These situations are difficult to confront, but they must be handled so that the rest of the organization can go about its business and achieve its mission. More commonly, however, the clashes occur between pairs of individuals who are good performers with a history of high performance in other situations. In this instance, moving one or both of the warring individuals often will solve the problem; frequently, they will seek the moves themselves. The system must accommodate such moves.

Movement between teams is also important to prevent them from stagnating. When the same people work together over the years, performing virtually the same function, they often cease to look for ways to improve. They become satisfied with their relationships, their roles, and their activities. Often, it takes an outsider, someone new to the team, to stir things up, ask questions, and propose new ways to improve results.

When you are looking for constant improvement, you must create an environment that nurtures such improvement. Static teams do not provide that environment. For this reason, it is not enough merely to *allow* people to move to other positions on other teams; you must somehow *encourage* them to make such moves.

Some organizations have done this by building assignments on multiple teams into a skill-based pay system. In other words, in any given team, there are only so many skills to acquire; to be of more value to the organization—and, hence, to increase their pay—workers must have skills on several teams.

A more subtle approach currently is used for management personnel in many organizations, whereby to be considered for higher and higher positions within management, an individual must have experience in a broad range of products or services, as well as several different functions. The motivation to move then becomes one of opportunity for promotion.

YOUR ROLE AS LEADER

Someone must be the champion of your new organization structure so that improvement can continue and your organization can meet the needs of all its constituents—clients, customers, shareholders, and employees. This responsibility falls to you as the organization's manager. Three traits that make a good leader, whether manager or entrepreneur, are also imperative for managing the optimized organization: the ability to create and communicate a vision, the ability to listen and respond to what you are hearing, and tolerance for ambiguity.

Adherence to the Vision

If your organization is to become and remain flexible, if people are to respond quickly to changing conditions, you cannot direct every activity and make every decision yourself. As a result, you must be certain that everyone understands and continues to understand the organization's mission and goals. You must operate by gaining commitment to a vision that is understandable and applicable across the entire organization.

To understand what I mean by vision, suppose that you are the manager of a five-person organization, based in Pittsburgh, whose mission is to beat a competitor's five-person crew to a checkpoint in Cleveland. Both your crew and your competitor's must drive the 100-mile distance.

In a traditional structure, you would load yourself and the four other people into a car and head for Cleveland with you at the wheel. You might ask others to navigate, provide entertaining conversation on the way, watch for traffic, or whatever, but all five of you would be traveling together, with you in charge. If the car broke down, all of you would be stuck on the highway. If you ran out of gas, none of you would make it to Cleveland.

In a more flexible, more responsive structure, you could break down the organization so that any member of your crew could reach Cleveland to check in and beat the competition. A victory by one would be a victory by all. As a responsible leader, you would explain the goal to each of the four other people and provide maps, compasses, and any other necessary resources. Each individual would then use his or her own ingenuity to reach the destination.

If, instead, you merely gave each of the four automobiles of their own and had them follow you down the highway without knowing where they are going or why, you would not be much better off than when you had everyone in the same car. In fact, you would consume far more resources—instead of one automobile traveling to Cleveland, you now have five, although only you know exactly where the group is going and why.

You can see from this illustration that visions are not mystical experiences but simply clear explanations of what must be done and why. They substitute for the reams of policies and procedures that may indicate exactly how things should be done but omit the whys and the results that must be achieved.

Creating and communicating a vision that is understood by all levels of the organization is perhaps your most important function in your newly structured organization. I have often had occasion to hear managers discuss their military backgrounds. Particularly interesting to me are those discussions between managers from different generations that contrast the American troops in World War II and the American troops in Vietnam. Ultimately, they generally agree that the biggest difference between the two conflicts was that, in World War II, U.S. troops clearly had a vision: They were going to win the war. No such clear-cut vision existed in Vietnam. It was this omission, many claim, and not the protests back home, that destroyed morale in Vietnam.

Ability to Listen and Respond

In order to be sure that your vision is understood and accepted by everyone in the organization, you must be able to hear what people are saying about their work, about the organization, and about the results that they are achieving. To do this, you must have excellent listening skills, and you must also know how to respond to what you are hearing.

If, for example, what you hear indicates that some people do not understand your vision, you must recognize that the responsibility for clarifying the vision is yours. If you react to the news that some people still are not in step with the organization by expressing anger, displeasure, frustration, or other negative emotions or actions, people may simply stop telling you what is happening. Losing this upward communication from the rest of the organization may be disastrous. Not only will you have no way of determining whether you have gained commitment to your vision, you will find it more difficult to build commitment where it is lacking, because you won't know where this is the case, and to sustain continued improvement, because no one will feel free to talk about where improvement is still needed.

The ongoing improvement process requires that you and every manager in your organization be receptive to feedback in all aspects of the organization's performance, including your own performance and behavior. As an example, consider a manager who wants to create an organization that is more flexible, with quicker response time. Such a change requires decisionmaking to be carried out at lower levels, but each time a decision is made, it is either reversed or criticized by the manager. The new structure cannot continue to provide quicker response time for long under these conditions. Eventually, people will learn that decisions need to be passed up the line if they want to avoid reprimands or criticism. In no time at all, flexibility and response time are back to what they were before the change. If the manager had been open to feedback, this situation would not have arisen, and the organization would indeed become more flexible and reduce its response time.

As the organization's leader, you must become the epitome of the good listener. You must set the example. Listening must become an activity that the organization values. Managers at all levels must be willing to listen to the feedback that they receive. Nonmanagers, too, must listen to feedback from other departments, other teams, their own team members, other individuals, and the customer.

The fundamental difference between an organization that is constantly improving and one that is stagnating is that the former learns from its mistakes, while the latter simply lives with them. Learning requires listening. There simply is no way around this imperative.

Tolerance for Ambiguity

I am not suggesting here that you have to enjoy ambiguity or even like it very much. But, in an organization that is learning and improving constantly, you must develop some tolerance for uncertainty. Only stagnant organizations can afford the luxury of having all the possible decisions made and all the contingency plans laid out before they deal with a given situation. In a constantly changing environment, few organizations can remain stagnant and survive. This means that, today and in the years ahead, no organization can remain successful if its leadership cannot tolerate uncertainty.

Tolerating ambiguity does not mean relying on serendipity to run your organization. Nor does it mean that you can couch the organization's mission in vague terms that can be interpreted a dozen different ways to suit changing conditions. Rather, it means depending on others to get the work done in the best way possible (which you probably do not have the time to spell out), constantly searching for ways to improve the organization, and encouraging others to do the same. It means recognizing that change is the only permanent condition that you can count on.

Sometimes, tolerating ambiguity may mean that, at any specific point in time, you may not be able to say exactly who is doing exactly what. Overall, you will know what groups of people have responsibility for which results, but the details may always be foggy. You will be busy communicating your vision and studying the results so that the overall organization can improve continually; you will not have time to manage details. In fact, if many of your managers still have time to manage details, you may have too many levels of managers. The people doing the work must attend to the details; your job is to provide them with the overall direction and the resources that they need.

CONCLUSION

As the manager of a continually improving organization, your leadership skills will need to include the ability to create and communicate a clear vision, the ability to listen and respond to what you hear, and the ability to tolerate uncertainty. In designing an organization for continuous improvement in the years ahead, you will discover that many contingencies cannot be anticipated in the early design stages. After the new organization is in place and all the supporting activities are aligned with the overall mission and structure, external conditions will change, and internal improvements will occur. As they do, changes must be made in your support systems.

The need for constant change to maintain a successful, optimum organization is likely to increase in the years ahead. Managers who wait to restructure their organizations until their environment and business conditions settle down are likely to be left in the dust raised as their competition pulls ahead of them. The unanswered questions that face your new organization should become guideposts for the future, rather than roadblocks for the present. Only by accepting continuous improvement and constant change as a way of life can you optimize your organization.

APPENDIX

GLOSSARY OF SOCIOTECHNICAL SYSTEMS TERMS

Never underestimate the power of words. In many cases, the terms, unusual and high-sounding, that are often used to describe and explain a sociotechnical systems approach have discouraged managers from applying the techniques. Some were invented, like *sociotechnical*, specifically to signify particular aspects to organizational design. I include them here only for those managers who enjoy words and may want to match vocabularies with a consultant who would be familiar with the vernacular. They also provide a review of the material within the book.

These terms are freely adapted from Albert Cherns (1976), who uses many of them to describe his principles of sociotechnical design.

Boundary location The divisions between the building blocks of the organization, particularly between teams. In a sociotechnical systems approach, teams should be responsible for whole tasks, products, or services. Often, the teams are separated from each other by the technologies involved in their tasks; the physical space or territory that people occupy to accomplish a given task, provide a service, or construct a product; or the fact that they work on different shifts or at different times. These three factors—technology, territory, and time—create what most experts consider to be natural divisions between teams.

Compatibility We discussed this aspect of sociotechnical systems design in Chapter 2, stating that the way you begin the change project should be congruent with the objectives that you are trying to achieve. For example, if you are trying to achieve greater flexibility, which requires more employee involvement, your change process should include as many people as possible in the initial stages of analysis and design. In Chapter 5, we described further how implementation must be congruent with the overall vision for the new structure.

Equifinality   The belief that a given outcome can be achieved equally well by a variety of approaches (see also "Multifunctional principle"). Automobile manufacturers who have moved from traditional assembly-line structures to semiautonomous work groups to build essentially the same product demonstrate this principle.

Incompletion   The notion that the final organizational structure probably will not be static. If you strive for continual improvement, you must be ready to modify your design as the need arises. If you discover, for example, that your initial ideas about how a part of the work should be organized are not working well, you must be willing to make changes. Even if your new design is perfect, environmental changes eventually will require adjustments to your organization so that it can remain competitive. Flexibility, by its very nature, requires constant adjustment. This concept was discussed in Chapter 8.

Information flow   In the ideal organization, information should be available to those who will use it. Particularly if you are looking for increased flexibility or shortened response time, you will be asking people at lower levels to make more decisions than they previously had been expected to make. They must have access to the information that they need—drawings, part numbers, material specifications, and so forth, but, especially, the overall vision of the organization's mission. The key to moving decision-making nearer to the point of action is to be sure that the decisionmakers are well-informed. We discussed in Chapter 7, for instance, the need to make appropriate measurements available to those who can use them best. In Chapter 2 and 5, we emphasized the importance of communicating the overall vision so that everyone understands where the organization is headed.

Joint optimization   Joint optimization is the heart and soul of a sociotechnical systems approach. The notion that both the people aspects and the technical aspects of your organization must fit each other is a departure from traditional organizational design, which tends to fit people around a particular technology as best it can. Designing an organization so that the social aspects and the technical aspects fit and complement each other is what optimizing the organization is all about.

Minimal critical specification   This mouthful of words simply means that no more should be specified in the new structure than is absolutely essential. In most cases, this means that, as manager, you will provide only the specifications for the results that organizational units should achieve; once they understand the results, the rationale, and their resource limitations, they will determine the details of how they will accomplish their goals. In other words, those who are most familiar with the work will decide how best to perform it.

Multifunctional principle   Some experts use the term "equifinality" to describe this principle. Both terms are puzzling, but the old adage that there is more than one way to skin a cat sums up the concept quite well. In Chapter 4, we examined this principle when we discussed how you can choose the type of design you want in your organization: whether you want teams of people who are mutually dependent on each other, units that are relatively independent of each other, or units that operate sequentially. The principle of equifinality or multifunctionality makes sociotechnical systems design one of the most flexible approaches to organizational structuring.

Sentient groups   Sometimes called "informal groups," these are the naturally forming social structures that often occur in organizations. Sentient groups recognize themselves as belonging together. One of the classic debates among sociotechnical systems theorists concerns whether formal task groups should be identical to sentient groups. Many argue that there should be some difference so that teams or groups do not become static and resistant to change. In Chapter 8, we discussed the need to encourage mobility between teams, which addresses this issue.

Sociotechnical criterion   The principle that variances, or unprogrammed events or problems, should be controlled as near to their point of origin as possible. Early in the analysis phase (see Chapter 3), variance tables or matrices are constructed so that you can see what kinds of problems or mistakes occur within the organization's operation, where they originate, and where they are discovered. Ideally, they should be discovered as close to their source as possible. This proximity allows people to receive feedback directly from their work, learn from their mistakes, and control their own quality.

Steady state   In order for an organization to remain competitive or have a consistent output in a turbulent environment, its internal operations must be capable of considerable flexibility. In other words, an organization must be capable of adjusting its processes continually to protect its results from the potentially negative effects of continual change in the environmental demands. The process by which an organization achieves a steady state is often called "homeostasis" or "dynamic equilibrium."

Support congruence   In Chapter 6, we discussed the need for supporting the new structure and the new behaviors that it requires. Reward systems, selection criteria, measurements, training, and policies and procedures are among the support systems that must be congruent with the organization's design and objectives.

BIBLIOGRAPHY

Bernstein, Aaron, and Wendy Zellner. 1987. "Detroit vs. the UAW: At Odds over Teamwork." *Business Week*, August 24, pp. 54–55.

Cherns, Albert. 1976. "The Principles of Sociotechnical Design." *Human Relations* 29, no. 8: 783–92.

Deci, Edward L. 1975. *Intrinsic Motivation*. New York: Plenum.

Emery, Fred E., and Eric L. Trist. 1978. "Analytical Model for Sociotechnical Systems." In *Sociotechnical Systems: A Sourcebook*, edited by W. A. Passmore and J. J. Sherwood, pp. 120–31. San Diego: University Associates, Inc.

Goldratt, Eliyahu M., and Jeff Cox. 1986. *The Goal: A Process of Ongoing Improvement*. Croton-on-Hudson, N.Y.: North River Press.

Hackman, J. Richard. 1977. "Work Design." In *Perspectives on Behavior in Organizations*, edited by J. Richard Hackman, Edward E. Lawler III, and Lyman Porter, pp. 242–56. New York: McGraw-Hill.

Hackman, J. R., and G. R. Oldham. 1980. *Work Redesign*. Reading, Mass.: Addison-Wesley.

Halberstam, David. 1986. *The Reckoning*. New York: William Morrow.

Herzberg, Frederick. 1966. *Work and the Nature of Man*. Cleveland: World Publishing.

Hoerr, John. 1986. "Management Discovers the Human Side of Automation." *Business Week*, September 29, pp. 70–75.

Iacocca, Lee (with William Novak). 1984. *Iacocca: An Autobiography*. New York: Bantam.

Jayaram, G. K. 1976. "Open Systems Planning." In *The Planning of Change*, edited by W. G. Bennis, K. D. Benne, R. Chin, and K. Corey, pp. 275–83. New York: Holt, Rinehart & Winston.

Kerr, Steven. 1975. "On the Folly of Rewarding A, While Hoping for B." *The Academy of Management Journal* 18, no. 4 (December): pp. 769–83.

Mitroff, Ian I. 1987. *Business NOT as Usual*. San Francisco: Jossey-Bass.

Morgan, Gareth. 1986. *Images of Organization*. Beverly Hills: Sage Publications.

—. 1980. "Paradigms, Metaphors and Puzzle Solving in Organization Theory." *Administrative Science Quarterly* 25, no. 4 (December): 605–22.

Peters, Thomas J., and Robert H. Waterman, Jr. 1982. *In Search of Excellence: Lessons from America's Best-Run Companies*. New York: Harper & Row.

Thompson, James D. 1967. *Organizations in Action*. New York: McGraw-Hill.

Tichy, Noel M. 1983. *Managing Strategic Change: Technical, Political and Cultural Dynamics*. New York: John Wiley & Sons.

Trist, Eric L., and K. W. Bamforth. 1951. "Social and Psychological Consequences of the Longwall Method of Coal-Getting." *Human Relations* 4, no. 1 (January): 6–38.

von Oech, Roger. 1983. *A Whack on the Side of the Head: How to Unlock Your Mind for Innovation*. New York: Warner Books.

Walton, Richard E. 1986. "From Control to Commitment in the Workplace." *Harvard Business Review* 63, no. 2 (March-April): 76–84.

Walton, Richard E., and Gerald I. Susman. 1987. "People Policies for the New Machines." *Harvard Business Review* 65, no. 2 (March-April): 98–106.

INDEX

and group structures, 103; the role of individuals in, 101–2; within/pooled between, 96–97, 107–8, 133

Research-and-development organizations, 90

Restructuring: and "building block" questions, 85; and "glue" questions, 85; last-resort approach to, 23, 56; the outcome of, expectations about, 25–28, 112; motivations for, 57; successful, determining the potential for, 22–24; timetable for, 23–24, 28

Retrofit situations, 53, 54–56; identification of options in, 65; selection in, 145–46

Reward systems, 4, 16, 98, 102; and continuous improvement, 157–60; and emphasis on customer service, 125; and emphasis on quality, 125; during the implementation phase, 119; and individual accountability to teams, 132; and poor organizational structure, 106; revision of, 123–36; and team accountability to the organization, 132–34; types of, 126–28. *See also* Compensation; Pay systems

Risk management, 22–23

Robots, impact of, on an organization, 13

Role clarification, 141–42

Rotation, of members between teams, 161–62

Rules, 145; in organizations with pooled relationships, 88, 92

Salaries, 98, 128, 129, 132

Savings-and-loan associations, 87, 88

Selection, 144–46

Semi-autonomous work groups, 27, 34

Sentient groups, 75, 76–77, 171

Service organizations, 90

Skill-based pay systems, 135

Skills, learning new, 142–44

Social needs, 104

Social structures, organizational, 75–80

Sociotechnical criterion, 171

Sociotechnical systems approach, 14–17, 123; application of a, at Volvo Corporation, 14–15; benefits of the, 5; four phases of the, 15–17; and

optimization, 22; the origins of the, 3–5; training employees to work with a, 42–44; use of a, in steel mills, 22; work design application of a, 14–15. *See also* Analysis phase; Decisionmaking phase; Follow-up phase; Implementation phase

Stagnation, and the division of labor, 11–12

Standards, 92–93

Status quo, maintenance of the, 25, 41

Steady state, 171–72

Steel mills, use of a sociotechnical systems approach in, 22

Steering groups, 47; and the analysis phase, 49, 66, 85; checklist for, 45; formation of, 39–44; and identifying problems, 66; and processing feedback, during the implementation phase, 119

Structures, organizational, 85, 86–98, 104–8. *See also* Relationships

Success: criteria for determining, 147; potential for, 22–24, 28

Supervisors, first-line, 77, 78. *See also* Management; Managers

Supervisory reports, 68

Suppliers, relationships with, 81–82

Support activities, 60, 80, 172

Support congruence, 172

Taylor, Frederick, 11, 101

Team membership, 157–58, 161–62

Team-oriented structures, 128, 129–31; budgets in, 138–39; and continuous improvement, 157–58; promotions in, 140; the role of managers in, 142. *See also* Groups; Teams

Teams, 27, 129–31, 141–42; accountability of, to the organization, 132–34; calculating the value added by, 130–31; competition between, 133; individual accountability to, 132; and measurement efforts, 154–55; problem solving in, 142–43, 154; rotation of members between, 161–62; and the selection of new employees in, 144–45; as units of analysis, 131–34. *See also* Groups; Team-oriented structures

ABOUT THE AUTHOR

Emily E. Schultheiss has over seventeen years of experience in manufacturing, human resources, organization development, and management training. She is currently manager of education and training services for Westinghouse Electric Corporation, headquartered in Pittsburgh, Pennsylvania.

Her interest in sociotechnical systems began in 1981, when she was asked to study the issue of robotics and make recommendations regarding their smooth integration into the workplace. Since then, she has worked with sociotechnical systems implementations in this country and abroad. Her current interests are in the area of preparing managers to be successful in the turbulent business environment of today and the coming decade.

She holds a B.B.A. in management from the University of Oklahoma, where she has served as a Distinguished Lecturer in the College of Business Administration, and an M.S. in human resource development from LaRoche College, where she received the first Distinguished Graduate Alumnus Award.